AMERICAN MIGHT
AND
SOVIET MYTH

by
Jameson G. Campaigne

HENRY REGNERY COMPANY
Chicago   1960

ACKNOWLEDGMENTS

To those who have helped make this book the kind of book it is:

Ferdinand L. Mayer, at whose suggestion it was written.

Jean Kellogg, whose perceptive editing and helpful suggestions are responsible for changes that greatly improved its quality.

Pierre Goodrich, whose interest and wise advice was of much help in the book's preparation.

And Edith, my wife, who suffered through more than forty lonely weekends, while I struggled to get the job done, without complaint and with wifely understanding.

First Printing September 1960
Second Printing December 1960

CONTENTS

FOREWORD

I believe every person who reads this book by Jameson G. Campaigne, the brilliant editor of the *Indianapolis Star*, will be moved to deep and serious thought.

Mr. Campaigne has directed this book to one facet of the ancient struggle of government against freedom. What he says in the following pages will be unpalatable to many. Obviously, he fears that the ideology of statism has infiltrated the stronghold of liberty. It is a belief which justifies anger. Seeming to oppose statism under one label while embracing it under another is a tragic irony. What Campaigne's book says to me is that we cannot promote the supremacy of the state in India or Turkey or Poland without wounding freedom in America. We cannot tolerate a self-serving bureaucracy in Washington without going part way down one of Mr. Khrushchev's many roads to Communism, which is, of course, statism. We cannot surrender to other less free nations one iota of the right to protect each American's freedom without erasing some of that freedom. These are things that need saying over and over and over, forcefully, even angrily. The debate they will provoke cannot but contribute to our understanding of the struggle in which we are engaged.

The author is a philosopher of a free society. He is noteworthy for his personal dedication to the cause of individual liberty. He has been articulate and emphatic in the defense of victims of discrimination against minorities, even when the victim was a minority of only one. He has brilliantly challenged the usurpation of authority by the United States Supreme Court. He has repeatedly exposed the dangers of an expanded Federal bureaucracy which feeds on bigger and more confiscatory taxes. In short, freedom is his business.

As editor of *The Indianapolis Star*, Jim Campaigne has brought the *Star* to national attention more than once with the defense of the downtrodden while others stood by uncomplainingly. A series of editorials on "The Runaway Court" dealing with the decisions of the United States Supreme Court during the last five or six years was reprinted in almost every state of the Union. More than a hundred thousand copies of these editorials were distributed through various persons who became interested in what Mr. Campaigne had to say. Just recently he completed a series of editorials on "The Power To Destroy," in which he reviews and exposes the fallacies of our Federal income tax structure.

Of Jim Campaigne I know this—what he writes comes from the heart as well as the mind.

EUGENE C. PULLIAM, PUBLISHER
The Indianapolis Star

CHAPTER I

LETTER TO THE READER

Who are you?

Are you a father working hard to provide for your family? Are you one of those men who do everything humanly possible to safeguard the future—taking out insurance to protect the children from sickness and accident, making plans for their education, paying into a pension fund towards the day of your own retirement?

Or are you a mother trying to teach your children to be everything you know they can be, sharing with your husband the plans he makes for them, looking forward to a life of accomplishment and to seeing your children and grandchildren grow up in the opportunities of a free society?

Are you a young man just starting out, full of enthusiasm and plans?

Are you a young girl, dreaming of marriage?

No matter who you are, you have the future ahead, a future for yourself and others for which you work and dream and plan.

But perhaps you don't realize this: Every dream you dream, every plan you make, all your work and worry can in one day come suddenly to nothing, if a few people sitting in offices in Washington—the people who direct the foreign policy of the United States—make one mistake too many.

Fifty or even twenty-five years ago, protected by the surrounding oceans, by the immense distances between us and any powerful foe, the people of the United States could almost disregard foreign policy. A mistake by our foreign-policy makers rarely led to anything more than a skirmish or a negligible loss of government funds. But today, this insularity has changed. Today, in a single terrible stroke, your home, your future, your children—your everything can be lost.

At one time, the conduct of foreign policy cost you virtually nothing in taxes. Today it takes 12 per cent of your income. If you earn $5,000 a year you pay an average of $491 in direct income taxes and $147 in other Federal taxes. You pay $105 in higher prices caused by the Federal taxes on everything you buy. Your share of the taxes paid by corporations who pay you dividends or other income is $68. So every year $811 is taken away from you to pay the expenses of your government. That is 16 per cent of your income.

Out of that $811.00 you pay in taxes, $629.13 goes to pay for departments or agencies directly or indirectly concerned with foreign affairs. In other words, 77 per cent of what you are forced to pay the Federal government is spent for foreign policy, past, present, and future —military defense, foreign aid, veterans payments, interest on the war-created debt.

Fifty years ago these things cost your grandfathers virtually nothing. Even twenty-five years ago it was an expense you hardly felt. Today, 10 per cent of your income goes for these purposes. And yet the United States is endangered as never before in its history.

Why is this so? It is so because those who have conducted the foreign policies of this country are failing you. Having involved you in the wars of 1917 and 1941, they lost the peace after you won the wars. They failed to recognize the significance of Hitler and Mussolini. They are failing to understand the policies of either Stalin or his successor Khrushchev. In doing so they fail you and your family. And because of these failures your life, your future, your country's very existence is menaced. Future failures can cost you everything that has made life in the United States the most rewarding ever lived by man on earth. They can cost you your life itself.

Your plans, your children's plans, now depend on whether or not those who conduct American foreign policy recapture success from present failure. Like a suspended sword of Damocles over your head, hangs the sword of American foreign policy.

For the first time in our history the people of the United States face the possibility of a war upon their own soil which could destroy our country and drive us into enslavement. Lincoln once said, "All the armies of Europe, Asia, and Africa combined, with all the treasure of the earth (our own excepted) in their military chest, with a Bonaparte for a commander, could not, by force, take a drink from the Ohio, or make a track on the Blue Ridge, in a trial of a thousand years. . . . If destruction be our lot, we must ourselves be its author and finisher. As a nation of free men, we must live through all time, or die by suicide."[1]

This is still true. Only by suicide can America die. But circumstances have changed since Lincoln's time, and in this era of the atomic bomb and guided missile, error and confusion in military and diplomatic leadership endanger us as never possible before. It is through our leaders that we may at last, in Lincoln's words, cause our own destruction, as no foreign commander could, even now.

It has been your habit as an American to leave foreign affairs to the "experts." But look at the mistakes the experts have made in China, in Korea, in Europe, in the Middle East. Today the security of the United States is in greater danger than it was ten years ago or even five. The so-called experts, who have taken your tax money

4

and made American foreign policy, have succeeded only in making your life less secure, your home less safe, and your freedom less certain than ever before in our history. Unless you assert your power as free men to change a foreign policy that has failed, that is failing, our nation may indeed soon die. It is as an attempt to simplify the issues of foreign policy so that every American can understand how closely his own life is affected by it, and therefore act to protect himself, that this book has been written. What is the fundamental problem that you face, and I face, as Americans living under the shadow of atomic war? There is only one threat. It is the menace of Communism spreading from its base in the Soviet Union to cover one third of the globe.

Because of the military threat of Soviet Communism we must spend $40,000,000,000 each year to defend ourselves. Because of Communism we send billions of dollars to seventy-six countries around the world. Because of Communism we build rockets and atomic submarines and air-craft carriers. Because of Communism we patrol the oceans and man bases at hundreds of points around the globe. Because of Communism we pour out our treasure and conscript our young men. Nothing else threatens this country. No nation in the Americas is a threat to us. No country in Europe could conceivably endanger our independence. No other country in Asia has the power to attack the United States. Only one country, Communist Russia, is our enemy, an enemy that could and will—if we relax—destroy us.

5

So the very first thing to understand about the foreign policy that affects your life and the lives of those you love, is "who is the enemy." When you know the enemy, then and only then can you defend yourself. The enemy is the Soviet Union, whose leader Khrushchev has said plainly, "We will bury you."

CHAPTER II

THE BATTLE FOR CHARACTER, HOW WE HAVE BEEN LOSING IT

Let us suppose you live in a small town. You are the leading citizen, known for your contributions to the library, to good government, to charity, and for your sound personal judgment and common sense.

One day you and your neighbors discover that termites have begun to infest your homes. Nobody in town knows much about termites, but your son, just back from college, has studied some entomology and he comes to you with a plan to get rid of the termites. He says he can do the job in four weeks. All he needs is $1,000 and the termites will be gone.

So you give him the $1,000 and he sets to work. First he buys exterminating equipment and hires people to operate it. Then he loans some of the money to your neighbors who are less well off, to help them get rid of termites. He tells you that the best way to get rid of termites is first to clean them out of neighbor Wong's house.

Then your son tells you that in order to get rid of the few termites you have in your house, which really are not serious at the moment, he must first get rid of them in everybody else's house in the neighborhood. He needs another $1,000 to exterminate them in the Bulls' house and the Frenches' house and some other homes down the block.

Nevertheless, after six weeks you quite clearly see that the termites are multiplying, not only around your house but all through the neighborhood. Your son tells you not to worry. He has been successful in keeping your house from falling down and other houses are still standing. All he needs is another $1,000, part of which he is going to use to buy feed for a new kind of pink termite which will fight against the dangerous red termites and make them weaker.

The pink termites, however, respond to this feeding by making big holes in your neighbors' foundations so that the red ones get in more easily. But, says your son, give him time and $1,000 more and the pink termites will turn on the red ones and everything will be fine.

Meanwhile the red termites have taken over the Lhasas' home, but your son doesn't mention that to you, and he decides that the best way to protect the Rhees' home and the Viets' home is to let the termites take half of each house, while he concentrates on merely trying to keep them out of the rest of it.

After two months he finally reports that this termite

invasion is obviously a permanent thing, and he will need $1,000 a week indefinitely to keep the termites from undermining you and all your neighbors. He remarks that after all, many houses are still standing, a fact which proves that his methods must be successful. Nothing whatever is said about his having told you in the beginning that he could do the whole job in four weeks with $1,000.

By now he has a big exterminator business going with a lot of people on his payroll and they have to be paid. Also the other neighbors, whose exterminating bills you have been paying right along because they are underprivileged and you are the leading citizen they rely on, have paid off their debts at the bank and are painting their homes.

At the end of twelve weeks the termites are worse than before, you are still spending $1,000 a week for termite control, and your son is still telling you that everything is going fine because only Wong's house and Lhasa's house have fallen down, Rhee's house and Viet's house are only half gone, the pink termites are bound to turn against the red termites someday, just you wait and see, and after all, the termites haven't destroyed the whole town yet, have they?

Meanwhile your banker feels it is necessary to pay you a call. He informs you that your checking account is overdrawn and there are rumors among the local merchants that your credit is not all that it used to be. In fact, your position as the town's leading citizen, which has enabled you in the past to do so much good, is in serious danger. He implores you to retrench, to make more money somehow, and set these matters right. You have always been so rich that he can scarcely believe that your assets are in their present deplorable condition. What would happen to the community without you?

In alarm, therefore, you invite the banker and the richer among your termite-infested neighbors to meet with you. You ask them to assist financially in the program of termite control. Politely they inform you that they are not financially able, but they also beg you not to abandon the program. For what would happen to them if you did?

Is this not a ridiculous story? It *is* ridiculous. But is it not exactly what American foreign policy, like the rich man's son, has been doing for, not the past twelve weeks, but the past twelve years?

The United States has been spending around $60,000,-000,000 each year for "termite control" against Communism. But during the past twelve years the termites have taken over China, half of Korea, half of Vietnam, all of Tibet. Although we have given millions of dollars in aid to the pink Tito termite and the pink Polish termite, they still are gnawing away on the same side as the Red Russian termite. Our national debt is at present larger than the national debts of all the nations in the world put together, while our allies nevertheless still refuse to provide enough troops and arms to defend themselves in Europe after ten years of financial assistance from us. Meanwhile the claims of foreign countries against the gold supply of the United States have driven down the total supply of American gold to only three billion above demand, though only two years ago the balance was nine billion.[1] The rapid fall has so undermined our international credit that sporadically even foreign investors, traditionally our best friends, get panicky, start withdrawing their monies, and look around for fresher fields.

General Eisenhower, when he was commanding NATO forces in Europe ten years ago said that if American troops were still in Europe ten years later, his mission of defense in Europe would have been a failure. In 1959 the tenth anniversary of NATO was celebrated and the U.S. 7th Army was the most powerful single force in Europe and was still on guard.

The past ten years have been a decade of foreign-policy failure for which the American people have paid a terrible price in lives lost and treasure spent. Yet today we are told that the Soviet Union is a greater danger than ever before. We are told that our past policies should be continued into the indefinite future, and that they are proved successful simply by the fact that we haven't had a war—yet.

Why do the people of the United States support a policy which in ten years has brought us to a situation which is still rightly described by Winston Churchill's words after World War II: "We lie in the grip of even worse perils than we have surmounted"? What is wrong with the makers of the American foreign policy? Why are they not successful in making your home more secure, your liberty more certain, your country stronger, and your enemy weaker?

What should foreign policy do? Secretary of State Dulles once said, "The purpose of the State Department is to look after the interests of the United States."[2] It is a statement with which no one can disagree. Therefore, what *are* our interests?

Our interests are national security, personal liberty, and national independence in order to perpetuate for ourselves and our children the life of individual opportunity which America has developed to a level unique in the history of the world.

These interests should come first in the minds of any government representing us in Washington. But do our makers of policy actually serve these interests? For example, when we deal with Nasser of Egypt and the United Arab Republic, what American interest is served by opposing the Arab attempt to achieve independence and union, an aim which arouses our instinctive sympathies as we remember our own revolutionary war? What American interest has been served by supporting exclusively British aims in Iraq on occasions which had nothing to do with American security or American liberty and often actually conflicted with American traditions of the liberty and self-determination of individuals and of nations?

12

Where American foreign policy has failed is where it has lost touch with its own past principles and ideals. For one hundred and eighteen years, from the time of Washington's farewell address until the outbreak of World War I, the United States followed a policy of trading and good relations with all nations, special alliances with none. It is fashionable today to sneer at the principles enunciated by Washington as unsuited to the atomic era. But these principles are in our blood. Our shunning of colonialism, imperialism, and all coercion of nations for selfish purposes, our historic detachment from "entangling alliances," our sympathy for all who seek freedom as we sought it, are part of our national image. They are the very essence of our identity as a people. Departure from these principles, which constitute our true character, has lost us more friends, made us more enemies, and done us more damage abroad than any other acts of our own in these two centuries of our existence. At one time our national image was cherished and clearly understood by most of the peoples in the world. Legends of the meaning of our revolution, of Washington who established a new nation, of Lincoln who freed the slaves, were the inspirational literature of young generations in every country on the globe. When actions represented to us as necessary to expediency and practical self-interest forced us to tarnish our authentic national image, there grew up among the world's peoples a belief that we were committing something like personal treason toward them all. And when one meets a foreigner who has this idea of us, it is hard indeed to prove to him that it is incorrect.

Therefore, these acts which were always sold to us by our leaders as expedient, as necessary to our self-preservation, are now turning out to have been in the long run about as inexpedient and as dangerous to our existence as they could possibly be. A world which once trusted us trusts no longer. Peoples once friendly to us look upon us as hypocrites.

But are we hypocrites? Is the accusation just? To nearly every one of us are not the principles of the Declaration of Independence still as sound today as they were a century and a half ago? Do we not still believe that all men are "endowed by their Creator with certain unalienable rights"?

In the earliest years of our existence we established certain principles in dealing with other governments. While history has made the application of these principles different in technique, it has not outmoded the principles themselves, nor can it permanently alienate them from our national character, without damaging that character beyond recovery or repair.

Said Washington:[3] "Observe good faith and justice toward all nations. Cultivate peace and harmony with all. Religion and morality enjoin this conduct. . . . It will be worthy of a free, enlightened and, at no distant period, a great nation to give to mankind the magnanimous and too novel example of a people always guided by an exalted justice and benevolence. Who can doubt that in the course of time and things the fruits of such a plan would richly repay any temporary advantages which might be lost by a steady adherence to it. . . .

"In the execution of such a plan nothing is more essential than that permanent, inveterate antipathies against particular nations and passionate attachments for others should be excluded, and that in place of them just and amicable feelings toward all should be cultivated. The nation which indulges toward another an habitual hatred or an habitual fondness is in some degree a slave. It is a slave to its animosity or to its affection, either of which is sufficient to lead it astray from its duty and its interest. . . .

"The nation prompted by ill will and resentment sometimes impels to war the government contrary to the best calculations of policy. The government sometimes participates in the national propensity, and adopts through passion what reason would reject. . . . The peace often, and sometimes the liberty, of nations has been the victim.

"So likewise, a passionate attachment of one nation for another produces a variety of evils. Sympathy for the favorite nation, facilitating the illusion of an imaginary common interest in cases where no real common interest exists, and infusing into one the enmities of the other, betrays the former into a participation in the quarrels and wars of the latter without adequate inducement or justification. It leads also to concessions to the favorite nation, of privileges denied to others, which is apt doubly to injure the nation making the concession by unnecessarily parting with what ought to have been retained, and by exciting jealousy, ill will and a disposition to retaliate in the parties from whom equal privileges are withheld; and it gives to ambitious, corrupted or deluded citizens, (who devote themselves to the favored nation) facility to betray or sacrifice the interests of their own country without odium, sometimes even with popularity, guilding with the appearances of a virtuous sense of obligation, a commendable deference for public opinion, or a laudable zeal for public good, the base or foolish compliances of ambition, corruption or infatuation. . . .

"The great rule of conduct for us in regard to foreign nations is, in extending our commercial relations to have with them as little political connection as possible. . . .

"If we remain one people, under an efficient government, the period is not too far off when we may defy material injury from external annoyance; when we may take such an attitude as will cause the neutrality we may at any time resolve upon to be scrupulously respected; when belligerent nations, under the impossibility of making acquisitions upon us, will not lightly hazard giving us provocation; when we may choose peace or war, as our interest, guided by justice, shall counsel. . . .

"Taking care always to keep ourselves by suitable establishments on a respectable defensive posture, we may safely trust to temporary alliances for extra-ordinary emergencies. . . .

"Even our commercial policy should hold an equal and

impartial hand . . . constantly keeping in view that it is folly in one nation to look for disinterested favors from another; that it must pay with a portion of its independence for whatever it may accept under that character; that by such acceptance it may place itself in the condition of having given equivalents for nominal favors, and yet of being reproached with ingratitude for not giving more. There can be no greater error than to expect or calculate upon real favors from nations. It is an illusion which experience must cure. . . ."

In considering this illusion which experience must cure, we have only to look back to the diplomatic and military developments seen by the generation that was born into World War I and lived through World War II and the Korean War. To many Americans, and to nearly all foreigners, the claim may seem astonishing, but it is an undeniable fact that the people of the United States, who gave their lives in two world wars within a quarter-century, did not deliberately enter either one. President Wilson was reelected on the slogan, "He kept us out of war." President Roosevelt's Chicago speech with its much repeated "I hate war" did more for his personal political cause at that time than any other statement.

Whether or not we should have entered these wars is now beyond discussion, since we did in fact enter them, with all our youth and treasure. However, we should at least note that the guilt for the climate which preceded both world wars, which made them both possible and probably inevitable, was partly of America's making and

depended upon an attitude which was in complete violation of our authentic character. In the years before
World War I, when the grievances and the power of im-
perial Germany were building, our diplomats went
quietly along with the foreign policies of England and
France. America was now becoming a world power and
we as a people were beginning to be swayed by the "passionate attachments" against which we had been warned.
Because of our admiration for Lafayette's France, and
our ties of blood with England, we stood implicitly at
their sides throughout that incredibly dangerous and ir-
responsible period when English and French statesmen
engineered the division of Europe into the two great systems of secret alliance. They finally exploded the century of peace and introduced the tragic era in which we
now live.

That was only a small beginning, however. Bound to
our wartime allies after World War I by attachments
grown far more passionate than before, we worked with
them to impose divisions of Europe and terms of peace
whose irrationality and vindictiveness are now regarded
as one of the outstanding follies in human history. Certainly it was the greatest possible departure from the
historic principle of justice toward all nations. And then,
when as a consequence of the poverty and bitterness
which grew after Versailles, the German people turned
to a pathological paranoid as to a savior, our own attachments grew deeper year by year. They were reinforced
by the state of mind which our national character had

once ruled out as most dangerous of all, "inveterate anti-pathies against particular nations." We saw the fascist dictatorships of Hitler, Mussolini, and Tojo. On the other side we saw the countries of England and France bound ever closer to us by ties of sympathy. The world was divided into black and white, with few shades of gray between them.

The fact that this view was naive and that its oversimplification drove us into the error of aiding the Soviet Union to reach the position it occupies today is by now so evident that few can be found to dispute it. In the 1930s, with the world regarded as separated into two opposing halves, the evil fascists and the good anti-fascists, there was no room for realistic appraisal of the Soviet Union. Facts which should have been obvious to every thinking person were obscured by the ever growing national psychology of passionate attachment coupled with inveterate antipathy. We completely lost that mental balance which we had begun to destroy in the years before World War I, but which had been both the essence of our national character and the greatest safeguard of our power to survive. When men of stature like Hoover or Lindbergh warned of the dangers, they seemed to most of America either to be talking nonsense or to appear to be semi-fascist themselves.

In that era, both men and events were, in the eyes of the average American, distorted out of all reality. To discuss whether our attachments and antipathies were justified is not the point. The point is that they developed in us a state of mind at variance with our traditions, whose sanity and clarity had brought us through two centuries to a pinnacle of freedom and personal happiness never before realized by citizens of any other nation. And they had caused nearly every other people in the world to look to us for hope and example. In the blindness of our mental climate after World War I, we followed our allies into policies which our historic position should have told us were dangerous, not only to our own national survival but to the entire Western world.

If you have any doubts about the violence done to our national character before and during World War II, read *Back Door to War* by Charles Callan Tansill[4] and *Wedemeyer Reports,* by General Albert C. Wedemeyer,[5] two men who are describing the facts of that era from experience. If you have any doubts as to the blindness after World War II caused by our antipathies and attachments, remember simply that the present isolation of Berlin is due to American orders. We deliberately held our armies back to allow Russians to advance. Remember too, that those same fatal few weeks also saw the orders which ruthlessly turned back into Russian hands hundreds of thousands of refugees pleading with the advancing Americans for the historic American rights of freedom and asylum. The fate of these tragic throngs who were turned back to the Russians is too sickening and too well known to need documenting here. But these acts are remembered by millions throughout Europe.

The image they hold of our national character has changed accordingly.

In whose interest were these things done? Were American policy makers putting American interests first when, before the eyes of watching Europe, they turned back the refugees to our "ally" the Russians? Or were they motivated by unreasoning drives, antipathies, and attachments, when they attempted, in the words of that period, to "cooperate with the Soviet Union"? What similar acts are taking place today, to which we allow ourselves to be blinded by attachments and antipathies peculiar to this era? Is it not time to be done at last with the attitude which has been so disastrous for us and for the world? Instead of letting ourselves be swayed by what purports to be "France's interest" or "Israel's interest" or "England's interest" or the "United Nations' interest" or even the so-called "interest of world peace," is it not time for us to return to our real character, and look to our own interest and to faith and justice toward all nations?

The plain fact is that today, in one crisis after another, the United States government works not for you, but for the specific interest of some other nation. Frequently it is a nation whose desperation or selfishness may be blinding it into misjudging what even its own interests actually are. Such is the case day after day with French colonial interest in Algeria; British and Israeli interest in the Middle East; British, French, and West German interest in Europe; Indian interest in Asia. In these areas policies are adopted which are directly contrary to the interests of the people of the United States, whose security, freedom, and national independence are at stake, should the course of action into which we are pressured by our allies fail to prevent Communist world domination.

A discerning columnist wrote not long ago, "Ours is an age of huddling. It highly regards 'collective defense' and it looks upon 'global responsibility' as greater than duties to home and country."[6] Actually there could be nothing more pernicious to true global responsibility than such an attitude.

We can add up the many times when America's best interest and best judgment have been sacrificed because our allies opposed what our leadership proposed, from the Berlin airlift, to the stalemated Korean War, to our bowing to British demands for summit meetings, to our support of British and French policies in the Middle East and Asia.

Even as late as 1949 if we had broken the Berlin blockade with a powerful show of strength at a time when we had a monopoly of atomic weapons and unchallengeably the mightiest army and navy in the world, there might now be no recurrent Berlin crises, for Berlin would be free. If we had won the Korean War, as General MacArthur and General Van Fleet and General Stratemeyer said we could have won it, again while we still had a monopoly of atomic weapons, Red China today might still be an impotent and revolt-torn nation. It is highly doubtful that Russia would at that time have entered any major conflict, and our decisive action then would have severely damaged Soviet prestige as an invincible threat. Korea would be united. There would be no divided Vietnam. Tibet would be free. And even the Soviet Union itself, having seen proof of our willingness to act with force and determination when necessary, might not have dared to march into Hungary while we, at the behest of our allies and the United Nations, stood by and weakly watched the crushing of the most glorious revolution for liberty in modern times. How terrible it will always be for Americans to remember the throngs in the last days of free Budapest, who marched up and down in front of our embassy, calling out, "Why don't you help us?"

In July 1958 the *Wall Street Journal* had an editorial which showed most eloquently the extent of our subjection to our allies. "So we reluctantly go to the summit," it said. "Things being as they are, it is probably the better course. But plainly it is a chastening reminder that 'what we do next' must be tempered, if not shaped, by foreign offices of other nations.

"The fact is that, whatever it may be, we are no longer master of our own foreign policy."[7]

It is because we are no longer master of our own foreign policy that our foreign policy no longer serves the interests of the people of the United States. It is also because we are no longer master of our own foreign policy that our foreign policy fails to give the people the successes they deserve for their sacrifices in three terrible wars.

When the United States has been successful in foreign policy since World War II, it has been only when we acted alone. Never when we acted upon the advice of or in concert with others.

What are our successes? The Truman Doctrine in Greece, when the United States, by its own decision and without consultation with others, sent General Van Fleet to Greece with weapons and funds, and defeated the attempted Communist coup in a matter of months, *without any reaction from the Soviet Union except verbal protest.*

The action in Iran right after the war when the Soviets threatened to take Azerbaijan. Prompt American reaction, and American reaction alone, drove the Soviets out. *They are still out.*

The unilateral decision to give quick military aid to Turkey, being threatened by Soviet forces, at the same time as the Greek threat. *The Soviets withdrew.*

In the same way, our entry into the Korean War could have brought success. We went in on our own. But before we could win that war, our allies and the United Nations, which we brought in with us, tied our hands and prevented victory.

On the other hand, when Red China threatened Quemoy and Matsu it was unilateral American action that stopped them. When our fleet moved into position, the Reds drew back.

Until the United States begins again to operate its own foreign policy in the interests of its own people, and to follow its own historic principles and to reestablish its authentic national character, it will continue to fail. The Soviet Union will continue to win the cold war. Until our policy becomes a United States policy, no United States government can hope to succeed in matching the determination and ruthlessness of the Soviet masters.

CHAPTER III

OUR FOREIGN AID:
HOW TO BE UNPOPULAR

In foreign lands they do not love us
Instead of hugging us, they shove us.
But one with even slight acumen
Can see that that is only human.
For being host and guest soon ends
The friendship of the best of friends.
RICHARD ARMOUR[1]

During the last ten years we have spent over $80,000,-
000,000 on foreign aid. Never has any nation poured out
so much treasure in the name of generosity. But has it
materially improved the lives of the people receiving it?
Suppose we take just one example, the foreign aid program to Lebanon, which I visited in 1957. A few instances of what we did in Lebanon may shed some light
on the present peculiar reactions abroad to our would-be
helpfulness.

We built an orange-sorting plant for Lebanese orange-growers. It has never been used. Why? Because no Lebanese orangegrower grows enough oranges to warrant the use of such a big plant for sorting. He sorts his produce in his own village and sends it to market himself. There are no cooperatives in Lebanon. Lebanese are fiercely individualistic and will not form organized groups—not voluntarily anyhow. Why didn't somebody point this out to the officials who planned the orange-sorting plant? But the officials might have had nothing to do if they had not built the plant. So the plant was built anyway, and there it sits arousing wonder and contempt as a monument to America's spendthrift inefficiency.

There was an earthquake in Lebanon and our government offered to help villagers rebuild their shattered houses. A program was started whereby the United States was to supply materials and technical help to show the Lebanese people how to rebuild their own dwellings. But when the money began to move, something happened. Instead of rebuilding the simple village homes, a housing project was erected. It was a splendid tribute to the vision of the building officials, who truly followed the American precept of "thinking big," but no Lebanese live in it. Why? It is not close enough to the villages where the people work. They cannot leave their jobs for homes so far away. So the houses sit empty, and the startled Lebanese have another monument to the peculiar character of the wealthy Americans.

That was not all, however. Housing soon became a stirring political issue in Lebanon. Several housing developments were planned. Whole areas were excited by promises of new housing. With the help of American funds, the Lebanese government embarked on a twenty-million-dollar suburban development on the outskirts of Bierut, Tripoli, Tyre, Sidon, and Zahle. A Greek engineer, famed for building at low cost, was brought in. The trouble was, however, that the people who were promised the housing did not live in Bierut, Tripoli, Tyre, Sidon, and Zahle. They lived in the villages in the mountains. In order to live in the housing projects they had to leave their villages and farms and become suburbanites. They had to get new jobs at higher wages because they no longer produced their own food on their own farms. Food production, of course, fell off as villagers left to flow into the new suburbs. Soon the whole economy of Lebanon was threatened by this unplanned, unreasonable, superimposed, and expensive project. Last spring I met in Washington two prominent Lebanese who had come to the capital to beg the United States please to stop giving their country foreign aid. The way things were turning out, it was ruining Lebanon.

Other American newspapermen have witnessed similar grotesque episodes. Eugene Pulliam, publisher of the *Indianapolis Star*, discovered the same sort of unthinking waste when he and his wife were reporting together from Turkey.[2] The politicians, seeking votes and publicity, had embarked on projects which did not mesh into the country's specific system. Thus with American funds they had unbalanced the economy, raised false hopes of economic improvement, and wasted American money, and among their more discriminating fellow-countrymen often aroused antagonism against America.

From Istanbul Mr. and Mrs. Pulliam wrote, "Prime Minister Menderes . . . has improved the roads in and around Istanbul, and the city itself. But in doing this he has demolished whole sections of the city, with no apparent plan for their replacement. The people who previously occupied these buildings are forced to seek homes elsewhere and they aren't to be found. No new dwellings are being built. . . .

"Another Menderes habit is to promise a new factory for the community he happens to be visiting at the moment. He has started hundreds of factories but has finished only a few. . . .

"A big sugar beet factory was built where there are only enough beets to keep it operating about eighteen days a year."

When good did result from American aid, it was often concealed from the people, whose politicians wanted sole credit. "A large amount of surplus food, drugs, and other commodities was released to the Turkish government for distribution among the needy. Menderes expressed his effusive thanks to the United States government, but did not allow a word about the receipt of the supplies to be printed in the Turkish press.

"Instead, the food and drugs and other articles were

distributed to the poor with a little card saying, in effect, 'This comes to you with the compliments of Menderes and the Democratic party.' The poor happened to live in the areas where Menderes wished to be sure of winning votes.

"The so-called land development program has degenerated into little more than a rich pork barrel for the supporters of Menderes. A high Turkish official told us of one man who qualified as a landowner. He received a million lire but had no land—not even one acre. So he built himself a villa, bought two Cadillacs on the black market, and had one swell time at the expense of the American taxpayer."

Vermont Royster,[3] Editor of the *Wall Street Journal* discovered the same conditions in Southeast Asia on a trip in 1959. Writing from Thailand he said: "Consider that here is a country which, for all that it may be backward by American standards, has managed to get along for one thousand years without the United States dollar aid or United States aid advisers. Its people are proud of their independence, their tradition, their own way of life, and are probably as successful in the pursuit of happiness as any people can be.

"Yet here come the Americans with a program which, when you look at it, would remake the country from one end to the other, from top to bottom. There is no area in Siamese life—schools, farms, business, language, homes, government, customs—left untouched.

"No one, be he a visitor here among the ancient tem-

30

ples and palaces or a stay at home reading about it, need be surprised that a program so conceived rubs many Siamese the wrong way. . . .

"One friendly Siamese . . . put it to his American visitor this way: 'I suppose we ought to be glad that you are helping us, but we do wish you wouldn't help us so hard.'"

The truth is that except for technical assistance, which is only a tiny part of the American aid program, mutual security aid, both military and economic, has often done far more harm than good. At the same time, by interfering with a nation's economic and even social life, American bureaucrats who are trying to Americanize the peoples of Thailand, Cambodia, or Lebanon end up by winning amused contempt or outright antipathy from the population.

Look at the world today. Has the foreign aid program won us allies? What new ones do we have? Has it won us respect and gratitude? Look at Bolivia, where the United States has financed the nationalization of Bolivian tin mines.[4] We started with $12,000,000 and six years later we had spent more than $152,000,000. The state-owned mines operate with an annual deficit of $10,000,000, which we make up. Production has fallen 50 per cent since they were socialized. Under Bolivian law, miners cannot be discharged. One mine, with work for only twelve hundred miners, has thirty-six hundred employees and loses $300,000 a year. The labor force could be cut by ten thousand men and operate more efficiently. Nationalized railroads, a program we also helped to foster, could operate more efficiently also with half their present employees. The cost of living in Bolivia, due to these practices, increased 200 per cent in 1956 alone, causing far more misery than the extra jobs in mines and railroads could possibly alleviate. Last year the Bolivians put on the most violent anti-American demonstrations in South American history.

The truth is that we are to blame, just as the Bolivian people suspect. We have subsidized inefficiency and made it unnecessary for their government to face up to the country's economic problems. By financing the stupidity and political ambition of Bolivia's socialist masters, we have incurred the animosity of her people.

In India, where our foreign aid enthusiasts claim their greatest successes, the real story is even more disheartening than the weird dramas of Bolivia and Lebanon. In England last fall I met a distinguished Indian economist, Dr. B. R. Shenoy, a professor from the University School of Social Scientists, Gujarat University, Ahmedabad. Dr. Shenoy described the American foreign aid program as the means for financing "the socialization and eventual communization of the entire country of India." He said that in the successive five year plans financed in part by United States aid, the Indian government is "creating a Communist type of economic structure that is paralyzing progress in agriculture, industry and business." In the first five year plan, "The amount of foreign aid was wholly used up in financing the export of foreign owned capital and in gold smuggling. Foreign aid, in other words, was in effect converted mainly into the dead assets of gold and partly exchanged for home assets owned by foreigners. It did not contribute to an augmentation of the national product, though the services charged on foreign aid are being drawn from the product." Dr. Shenoy said, "To the extent foreign aid does not add to the capital base, the economic ability to repay the debt is not being built up. This raises the important question, whether foreign aid, in a background of domestic inflation and basic economic disorders, is in the best interests of the giver and of the receiving country."

Foreign aid is helping a socialist Indian government finance the collectivization of agriculture. Strict socialist controls have throttled business and industry. As a result, according to Dr. Shenoy, "The Indian citizen at the close of two years of the second plan was poorer than he was at the close of the first plan." As in Lebanon, Laos, Turkey, and Vietnam, the foreign aid program in India is disrupting the natural flow of the economy and causing new problems instead of solving old ones. "The greatest foreign aid you can give to India," concluded Dr. Shenoy, "is the philosophy of economic freedom that has created . . . America's tremendous industrial and agricultural progress."

All over the world this same pattern appears. In Iran we built a road which goes nowhere and sank money into a dam which in the end was never built. In Latin America and the Middle East, anti-Americanism is rising, not in spite of our foreign aid programs but because of them.

On June 26, 1958, the House Committee on Government Operations concluded ruefully, "The administration of major construction projects in the foreign aid program, by the International Cooperation Administration, has been inadequate, indifferent and incompetent. . . . As a consequence, the achievement of the objectives of foreign aid has been impeded, and the dignity and prestige of the United States government abroad have suffered."[5] No informed or thoughtful person can fail to agree that our prestige has suffered. The aspect of our character indicated by our bungling foreign aid both bewilders and distresses our friends abroad. Says Malcolm Muggeridge, British newsman and television commentator, "The great puzzle about America to me has always been the contrast between its amazing economic vitality and its cumbersome government and administration. . . . There is so much energy and initiative in factories, offices and farms and so little in the State Department. In America everything seems to work except the administration."[6]

When one compares the success abroad of American industry with the failures of American diplomacy, the central cause of both is immediately evident. If American businesses abroad are inefficient they go broke. They must make a profit or they will perish. So they learn to do the things which will enable them to avoid that penalty. But when American diplomacy fails, there is no penalty for American diplomats as there is for American businessmen. The State Department just secures another appropriation.

The inefficiency of our foreign aid is not, however, its most disheartening failure. Nor is even its waste of American money, or the hostility and misunderstanding it has roused against us. To anyone who studies our foreign aid, the worst aspect is that he must soon suspect the entire program was based on false premises. We were told that foreign aid, by fighting poverty, would fight Commu- that it would keep newly independent nations free, that it would keep Communists away from underdeveloped areas. We were told foreign aid would keep us out of war, and was necessary to keep American workers employed and the United States economy strong. We were told that foreign aid, by fighting poverty, would fight Commu- nism, which thrives on poverty. And because we did in fact not have a war, and American workers were fully employed, and our economy remained outwardly strong, and Western Europe did not turn to Communism, and there still are underdeveloped areas where the Commu- nists have not taken over, it was assumed that the case for the foreign aid program was proved.

Today, however, no person who examines the actual facts can still believe the claims of proof are any proof at all.

How have the Communists made their gains? How did they win control of Eastern Europe? Did poverty turn the Eastern Europeans to Communism? Not pov- erty but the Soviet troops, who forcibly occupied these areas after World War II, made Eastern Europe Communist. The United States gave many of these communized nations foreign aid right after the war, perhaps the most going to Poland. The plain fact is that the Communist overlords took United States foreign aid and used it to reinforce their iron control over oppressed and unwilling peoples. In Eastern Europe poverty had nothing to do with the rise of Communism. In the whole of Eastern Europe before and during the war there was only one strong Communist party. It was in prosperous Czechoslovakia. In the poor Balkans, Communism had no hold at all, until it was established by military force. The supposed correlation between poverty and Communism is badly shattered when one looks at the facts.

In Western Europe today the strongest Communist parties are in France and Italy. In Italy the Party is strongest in the northern industrial areas, whose living standards are much higher than in the south, where there is virtually no Communism. In France the Communists are strongest in the cities and weakest in the countryside, where the poor peasants live. In Greece the United States has been most generous with its foreign aid, and the Greek national economy has greatly improved. Yet in 1958 the Communists in Greece increased their vote by 300 per cent and their representation in parliament from seventeen to seventy-eight. The Communists have the second largest party in Greece, now that Greece is more prosperous.

We have been pouring aid into India at the rate of

around $235,000,000 a year. Yet from 1952 to 1957 the Indian Communist Party increased from four million members to twelve million and is today India's second largest party. The Communists won temporary control of the Indian state of Kerala, which is not only one of India's more prosperous states but also has the highest literacy rate. Not only the supposed correlation of Communism with poverty, but its correlation with illiteracy now becomes highly suspect.

What is the poorest nation in Western Europe today? It is Ireland. Yet Ireland has practically no Communists at all. Communists have no organization in Ireland because they lack minimum support. And Ireland receives not one penny from the United States in foreign aid.

Did foreign aid save Western Europe from Communism? Eric Johnston, chief spokesman for the Committee for International Growth, always in favor of more foreign aid, has publicly stated that the Marshall Plan saved Western Europe when it was in imminent danger of falling into Communist hands in 1948. But what are the facts?

In the first place, the Marshall Plan was not even aimed at combatting Communism. It was offered not only to Europe but to the Soviet Union itself! General Marshall explicitly said that his plan "was not directed against any country or any doctrine."[7] It was to aid restoration of war-torn economies throughout the world. The Soviet Union refused Marshall Plan aid and also prevented its captive states from accepting it.

37

In the second place, Communists were no longer dangerous in France and Italy when the Marshall Plan went into effect. In 1947, one year before the Marshall Plan, the French had succeeded in barring Communists from any effective part in French government. In May 1947, Italian Premier De Gasperi expelled the Communist members of his cabinet and defeated the Communist inspired political strikes.

Those who claim success for our foreign aid programs make much of the fact that foreign aid has drawn Communist dictator Tito out of the Soviet orbit. But what is the fact? The fact is that Tito broke with Stalin a year before he received any aid from us. Nor did any promise of aid influence him. Between September 1947 and March 1948, he was expelled from the Comintern, and he turned his back, temporarily, on Stalin. The quarrel was primarily over Soviet draining of the Yugoslav economy, and variations between Soviet and Yugoslav applications of Marxism. American aid had nothing to do with it. In fact, the United States was on bad terms with Yugoslavia at that time because Tito's planes had just shot down an American plane over Yugoslavia.

When were Tito's relations with Khrushchev at their best? The interlude of warm understanding between Khrushchev and Tito was building up precisely during the months when Tito was receiving generous aid from the United States, and it was when United States aid began to decrease that Tito had another break with the

Kremlin. Our aid to Tito clearly had nothing at all to do with Tito's on-again-off-again relationship with Moscow. What $800,000,000 in American aid actually did was only to enable him better to fasten iron control on the Yugoslav people.

Let us leave Europe and consider the Middle East. Iraq got all her foreign aid from the United States and Great Britain. Egypt got most of hers from the Soviet Union. Yet Iraq is now nearly under the control of Communism, while Egypt is the strongest opponent of Communism in that area today. Our foreign aid did not keep Iraq from being pro-Communist. Communist foreign aid did not keep Egypt from being powerfully anti-Communist.

Foreign aid has proved to have no relation to the rise and spread of Communism. But still the myth persists, and still we pay out $6,000,000,000 a year, on the average, for a foreign aid program that is sold to us as efficient because its proponents say it has efficiently been fighting Communism.

The most ludicrous aspect of all is that, if foreign aid is supposed to fight Communism, why are we giving foreign aid to Communist countries? According to the Library of Congress, we gave $17,723,000 "mutual security aid" to Communist Hungary between 1955 and 1957. In 1957 alone we sent $10,166,000. Thus in that year we rewarded the Communist Kadar government for suppressing with Russian troops the people's struggle for freedom. Thus we relieved the Soviet Union of the necessity of supplying that amount to Hungary. Is this "fighting Communism"!

From 1954 to 1957 we gave East Germany $17,339,-000. Do we fight Communism by economic aid to Communist overlords of an enslaved people?

We have given strongly anti-Communist Spain a total of $241,000,000 since World War II, but we have given wholly Communist-controlled Yugoslavia $780,000,000 in the same period. Obviously, the foreign aid program for these two countries made it seem far more profitable to be Communist than anti-Communist. What remotest relation does such apportionment have to "good faith and justice to all nations"?

Of course the proponents of our present foreign aid program never sold it to us as an issue of principle such as justice or good faith. It has been sold on the basis of practical expediency as an efficient fighter of Communism (which we have seen it is not) and as a benefit to ourselves to strengthen our economy. Yet it has never been demonstrated that the foreign aid program has ever done anything actually to benefit the people of the United States. It has cost us more than $80,000,000,000, or an average of more than $2,500 per United States citizen over a ten-year period. Did you get your $2,500 of benefit over those years?

Senator Byrd, a constantly alert observer of foreign aid, has said: "The most dangerous of all myths is the belief that foreign aid is a substitute for a vigorous and realistic American foreign policy. . . . Today our foreign aid program is not an effective instrument of a carefully conceived foreign policy. . . . Foreign aid just keeps rolling along the same old lines, although the foreign policy problems have changed substantially in the last decade. As it rolls along, the layers of mythology get thicker and thicker, hiding from our view the underlying realities."[8]

The realities are:

1. The immensely expensive government-to-government foreign aid program has not only drained the financial resources we need to keep ourselves strong and caused our gold reserves to fall to their lowest ebb in years, but has also dropped America from her world position as a respected and beloved nation to a level of dislike and active distrust which we have never before had to face.

2. It has harmed countries receiving aid:

(a) in several cases by assisting dictatorships in fastening a tighter grip on subjected and unwilling peoples;

(b) in many cases by allowing governments to postpone facing economic problems which must eventually be solved from within;

(c) in nearly all cases by disrupting the economies of recipient nations.

3. This program, which has been praised as the most effective mode of fighting Communism, can now be seen to have had no correlation with the rise and spread of Communism as it has actually taken place

since the foreign aid program was instituted. Our foreign aid, wasteful, inefficient, beset with graft and bureaucratic confusion, has taken these characteristics with it into the countries where it has been applied. Graft and bureaucratic waste are not characteristics which impede the rise of Communism. They are precisely the characteristics which encourage it.

Our foreign aid government-to-government program does not work, has not worked, and cannot work.

CHAPTER IV

HOW NOT TO WIN AN
ELECTION IN LAOS

Even some Americans who opposed many aspects of the foreign aid program believed that the 1958 best-selling book, *The Ugly American,* must exaggerate our errors. The book was fiction and its authors, William J. Lederer and Eugene Burdick, told a story of mismanagement, carelessness, stupidity, and lack of understanding of the languages and cultures of Asian nations that was appalling—and, to some readers, unbelievable.

But in June, 1959, quite another type of book was issued concerning our foreign aid in Southeast Asia and came to the same conclusions. This book was titled *Seventh Report by the Committee on Government Operations of the House of Representatives.* Its subject was *U.S. Aid Operations in Laos,* a report of fact, not a work of fiction.

Laos is a small country north and east of Thailand or

Siam. Since World War II the United States has, through 1958, spent $150,861,000 on "mutual security" plus nearly $1,000,000 more on other activities. Laos is the only country in the world where the United States pays 100 per cent of the military budget. The committee report starts off with conclusions from long and painstaking investigation:

"1. Giving Laos more foreign aid than its economy could absorb, hindered rather than helped the accomplishment of the objectives of the mutual security program.

"2. Excessive *cash grants* forced money into Laos economy at a faster rate than it could be absorbed, causing:

(a) An excessive Lao government foreign exchange reserve, reaching at one point $40,000,000, equal to a year's aid.

(b) Inflation, doubling the cost of living from 1953 to 1958.

(c) Profiteering through import licenses and false invoices, which made possible the purchase of U.S. grant dollars for 35 kip (Laos currency). These dollars could be resold on the free market for as much as 110 kip.

"3. Much of the overspending is the direct result of a determination to maintain a 25,000 man Lao army. . . .

"In Laos . . . the decision to support a 25,000 man army with U.S. aid funds was made by the Department of State, despite contrary recommendations by the Joint

Chiefs of Staff. This was a political decision in a military field. There is no evidence that it was essential to support a 25,000 man army. . . ."

"4. A basic difficulty—undermining the success of the aid program in many ways and giving rise to the evils of speculation, profiteering and corruption—was the artificial and unrealistic 'official' rate of exchange of 35 kip to the dollar, whereas the free market rate soared as high as 110. . . .

"5. The concentration of benefits of the aid program to the area around Vientiane and other centers of population, and the enrichment of, and speculation by, Lao merchants and public officials, tended to lend credence to the Communist allegation that the Royal Lao Government was 'corrupt' and 'indifferent' to the needs of the people."

These are direct quotations from the committee's report. The rest of it reads like fiction, far more unbelievable than the story in *The Ugly American*.

First, Lao officials, for reasons of their own, decided to raise the pay of the army by $2,800,000. They did not consult United States Ambassador J. Graham Parsons. Even when the ambassador found out, however, he made no protest. He merely agreed to the raise, though it would obviously bring army pay to a scale far higher than the wage levels of surrounding areas and cause drastic inflation and hardship. In January 1959 another $1,000,-000 raise was granted. So far the army raises alone have cost the United States $10,000,000. The second raise was

45

proposed to Washington through the new ambassador, Horace Smith. It was rejected by the United States authorities in Washington. But the Lao government put it into effect anyway, and the State Department and International Cooperation Administration officials weakly passed it on the ground that "commitments had already been made."

The committee's report reveals that aid funds were also turned over directly to the Lao government for special projects. The Lao government deposited an equal amount of kip at the rate of thirty-five to one dollar. The aim of thus handling the United States aid was "to limit inflation." But "so unsuccessful has this system been that the cost of living in Laos doubled between 1953 and 1958."

Another reason for handling the money this way was ostensibly to stimulate local investment in local industry and business. The reverse happened. "Excessive use of cash grants and related laxity in import controls have, in effect, led to the financing of *capital flight* by the United States aid program, in a country where one of the primary needs is for local investment capital." Instead of helping Laos, foreign aid actually did great harm to the economy.

Meanwhile, back in Washington, the ICA had heard from six separate sources about this type of policy failure. Howell and Company, a management consulting firm, was sent to Laos. The Howell group recommended drastic changes to save money. But "Howell's tenacity in bringing embarrassing facts to the attention of the mission did not enhance his popularity. . . . The Royal Lao government . . . requested the continued services of the Howell group. . . . ICA/Washington, however, decided that no funds were available for this purpose. Their contract was not renewed."

Next came the Sessions group, from ICA, Department of State and Defense. This second group recommended that the "time has come to put the Laos aid program on a sound basis and reduce the United States aid level." Its key recommendation was that the mission director Carter dePaul be removed because, "The principal organizational weakness in USOM (United States Overseas Mission) is its lack of adequate direction." In spite of this finding, however, Carter dePaul (of whom more later) stayed on for fourteen months and was then promoted to be Deputy Assistant to the Director on Matters Concerning the National Security Council, the Operations Coordinating Board, and the Committee on Foreign Economic Policy.

Then there was Haynes Miller. He was an ICA "end-use auditor" assigned to Laos. His assignment was to check the use of the commodities, equipment, and funds in the aid program. He began examining the use of equipment for road building by the Universal Construction Company which had contracts with the mission.

"Miller concluded that ninety-four per cent of the equipment examined by him . . . was unsatisfactory in condition or use or both." He then began to get into other aspects of the aid program and reported misuse of funds and equipment to USOM Controller Harry Harting. Harting and his deputy, Norman Koltz, tried "to suppress the report and it was finally released only after his [Miller's] expressed intentions to bring the matter to the attention of ICA/Washington. The conclusion is inescapable that Haynes Miller was 'railroaded' out of Laos because he was close to discovering the truth about Universal, its bribes, its virtual monopoly of United States construction projects in Laos, and its woefully inadequate performance. The prime mover in ousting Miller was USOM Director Carl Robbins, acting on the basis of his confidence in Edward T. McNamara and the USOM Controller Harry Harting. Ambassador Parsons abetted this removal and loaned it the color of his name and office."

Ambassador Parsons did more. He sent a telegram to the Department of State which "cannot be quoted verbatim for reasons of communications security" which said Miller should be removed. He recommended the removal "because of obvious signs of nervous disorder," and because he "associated with low French," some of whom "are opium addicts and scorned by other French." The committee report notes that the ambassador's charge of "nervous disorder" was "rendered without benefit of medical advice" and "is contrary to Department of State regulations"—a fact which obviously, however, did not save Miller.

The committee report states flatly that Miller's detractors "were more interested in proving him wrong than they were in determining the existence of deficiencies in the Laos program." And the fact is that Miller was a top-flight career man. His removal from the mission was, in the opinion of the committee, "based on an undefined catch phrase, 'unable to adjust.' It appears to the committee that, if this refers to Miller's ability to adjust to the environment in Laos, it is grossly inaccurate. He was one of the few qualified French linguists in the mission, probably the most linguistically competent of the American employees. He was also, on the testimony of a number of witnesses, the one who, on a social basis—and with a real wish to 'adjust'—most sought the company of Lao and French nationals"—the "low French" disdainfully referred to in the report. In other words, Miller tried to work and live and associate with the people of Laos. He spoke their language and tried to understand their way of life. For this, and for the finding of corruption and thievery in the United States aid program, he was forced to leave.

And, though Miller's reports were sent on to ICA/Washington, "It is not apparent that ICA/Washington any more than USOM Laos, made any use of the information obtained from Miller."

If ICA/Washington had followed up Miller's reports what would they have found?

They would have found that Edward T. McNamara, the previously mentioned public works and industry officer for USOM/Laos, was bribed by the Universal

Construction Company for awarding and approving its contracts in Laos. "In return for these favors, he received from Universal, money, stocks, and airline tickets totalling at least $13,000. This he has admitted under oath." Note that these facts were uncovered directly by the committee, not by ICA. The McNamara case had been closed by the ICA before the committee commenced investigating it.

"The reason for closing the case, apparently, was that McNamara had left ICA's employ. The personnel security and integrity investigator assigned to the matter testified that he 'did not know where he [McNamara] was.'" It does not seem that McNamara should have been hard to find. He was a block away from ICA/Washington headquarters, employed by the firm of Transportation Consultants Inc., headed by General Lacey V. Murrow. And Transportation Consultants Inc. was "under an engineering contract with USOM/Laos." Obviously ICA did not concern itself with corruption as long as the corruption was able to escape notice. Nevertheless, to have McNamara a block away with another construction company, also under contract to USOM, does seem rather close quarters. Americans who pay taxes may meditate with some bitterness on the activities of the Universal Construction Company.

And how many more programs would reveal the same graft, the same corruption, the same waste, the same stupidity, the same cover-up, the same total disregard for the money and the prestige of the United States?

The Laos case illustrates far more than corruption, however. It tellingly lays bare the sort of incident which so dangerously destroys American character in the eyes of the people in precisely those areas where our enemies are most active.

For example, Carter dePaul, who headed the mission and whose abilities, as we noted earlier, were questioned by the Sessions group, sold his ten-year-old Cadillac, with his record player thrown in, to Universal Construction Company for 120,000 kip. The car was subsequently cut in pieces and dropped down a well, because the sale became known and embarrassing questions were being asked. "Our Embassy in Laos converted 106,530 kip of these proceeds for dePaul into $3,038, representing payment to dePaul of about three times the amount he could have obtained in the open market." It is easy to envision the reaction of Laotians who observed the sort of man dePaul was, and noted his subsequent promotion.

A plan to build twenty-five houses for ICA employees was disapproved by a member of the Howell group. He said a windfall exchange profit of $50,000 would be made, that the location was poor and that "the entire group of promoters had no demonstrable ability to complete the construction." Nevertheless, for reasons that need only be imagined, the contract was approved. The houses were started. The builders went broke. Mr. dePaul tried to get approval to repair the houses, still unfinished. Cost of repair was estimated at over $300,000. His successor found them in very bad condition and that to complete them would be an "economic nightmare." Another group of twelve houses, built at the cost of $30,000 each, was located in a saucer-like area, without any natural drainage. "In the wet season . . . it became a mill pond and the accumulation of water was so serious that the residents were reduced to wearing boots and using boats. Moreover . . . each house had been costing the government over $300 a month for maintenance alone." One may imagine the puzzled people of Laos observing the abandoned houses, and $30,000 homes drowning in the "mill pond."

You will remember that it is the stated purpose of foreign aid to "raise living standards" and create economic stability in order to prevent the Communists from gaining ground in "backward countries."

In May, 1958, special elections were to be held in Laos to fill twenty-one seats in the national assembly. In the fall of 1957 Ambassador Parsons decided to use the supposed power of United States foreign aid to help the anti-Communists in Laos win the election. Reported the committee, he "contemplated the cumulative results of the United States program to date. He was concerned with the possibility that its shortcomings might become election issues for the Communists. He was apparently impressed by the aid program's obvious neglect of the needs of the typical Lao, the rural villager or farmer. In an effort to remedy this shortcoming, the Ambassador conceived Operation Booster Shot." Over $400,000 in reported aid was spent by this program to defeat the Communists in the election. The committee estimated that a further total of at least $3,000,000 was spent in airplane drops of equipment and in stocks of American goods. More than ninety work projects, "including well digging, erection of small irrigation and flood control dams, repair of schools and temples, repair of roads and airfields and construction of hospitals, and the dropping of thirteen hundred tons of food, medical and construction supplies and other useful commodities" was involved. Here, indeed was a classic example of the real aims of the United States foreign aid—"people to people," as it has been called. Here is what all proponents of the program claim we must do to fight Communism in "backward nations."

Testifying before the House Foreign Affairs Committee in May, 1958, Ambassador J. Graham Parsons "foresaw a future in which the Communists would lose their two Cabinet seats, and the RLF [Royal Lao Government] would have gained two northern provinces [from the Communists] without bloodshed or any actual concession."

What actually happened? "The election was a Communist victory"! "Of the 21 contested seats the Communists won 9 and their sympathizers 4." The committee report goes on to state the obvious: "The aid program has not prevented the spread of Communism in Laos. In fact, the Communist victory in last year's elections, based on slogans of 'government corruption' and 'government indifference' might lead one to conclude that the

United States aid program has contributed to an atmosphere in which the ordinary people of Laos question the value of the friendship of the United States." In plainer words, *American foreign aid in Laos was responsible for wide Communist victories in Laos.*

In addition to the election failure, Ambassador Parsons, unable to "remove the Communists from the northern provinces by diplomatic pressure or military force," brought about "a compromise solution which admitted Communists to the government and which established the Communist Party, Neo Lao Hak Xat, as a legal, aboveground political party"!

The Lao government, last year, was forced to adopt dictatorial methods and expel the Communist cabinet members, but the Communist Party is still powerful in Laos. After reviewing the evidence, do we not feel that we now understand cogent reasons for Communism's continued and no doubt growing power?

And yet for this, we Americans, you and I, spent around $350,000,000 of our tax dollars in Laos.

In considering the problem of the $350,000,000, the flooded houses, the overpaid army, the Communist-won election, and the government's subsequent introduction of repressive measures, we might do well to stop a moment and look at this picture as a whole. Is there not something vaguely familiar about it?

Communist propaganda has labored unremittingly to destroy the images of America which have been in the minds of peoples everywhere—the land of Lincoln who freed the slaves, of Washington who fathered the new nation. There is an incessant propaganda battle to replace this image with another: America, the nation of plutocratic wealth and corruption, of profiteers with gangster mentality, who, for the purpose of exploiting the world's peoples, are in sinister imperialistic alliance with repressive governments, usually kept in power by the might of the army against the will of the population. If the outward appearances in Laos had been deliberately designed to fit the Soviet strategists' false image of the United States, we could scarcely have put on a better display.

The hero of *The Ugly American,* in the novel of that name, lived among the people. He did not surround himself with servants and sure-to-be-envied luxury, and he did not associate with rulers and princes. He built no roads to nowhere and started no dams that were never finished. What he did was establish efficient village-based light industry which enabled the people of the locality to work out their own prosperity. Fortunately for the United States, this sort of American is not wholly a fictitious character. He exists. There are perhaps a few hundred of him scattered around the globe—agriculturalists, cattlemen, experts in small industry, teachers, doctors. Dr. Tom Dooley wages war on disease in Laos and Thailand; Eugene Hoops fights topsoil erosion in Korea; Paul Rusch raises cattle on a bitter hillside in Japan; Mrs. W. H. Fisher combats illiteracy in India. Intelligent grants for such men and women, whose funds usually now must come from private sources, would make a great deal more sense than the astronomical official payrolls weighted with free-loaders.

Let us take just a moment to see what a typical enterprise of this kind is like—who heads it and how it gets started. A good example is Paul Rusch,[1] a humane man with a liking for people and an itch for accomplishment, who got into his work almost by accident. In Japan before the war, he was a teacher at Tokyo University. When Japan attacked the United States at Pearl Harbor, Rusch together with other Americans who had been living in Japan, was put into a concentration camp. After a time he was exchanged, and he returned to Japan after the war as an officer in the American army. Many Japanese, puzzled and shocked by their country's defeat, were curious about other ways of life than their own, and some of Rusch's former students who got in touch with him began to question him about America, its philosophy and way of life, and particularly the meaning of democracy. To Rusch, explaining these things meant delving back into the origins of our history. He told how the Pilgrims had banded together against the wilderness of the new world, how they had learned to govern themselves through an improvised system of small public meetings, and how they had become accustomed to helping one another through the necessary exchange of labor required to build each other's barns and cabins. He told how the Pilgrims developed the attitude which was particularly American and which has grown continually—an attitude of neighborly helpfulness combined with firm self-reliance on both sides. Don't let other people run things for you, was the burden of Rusch's plea. Do it yourselves. If Communists, or Americans, or even a single class of your own people like the Samurai run things for you, the result is not good for the country—and it is certainly not "democracy."

Out of this kind of discussion, Rusch and some of his Japanese friends began to develop a sense of purpose. Japan's fertile land was intensely cultivated, but fertile land is only sixteen per cent of the total. Eighty-four per cent was virtually unused. To Rusch it seemed perfectly clear that there was an immense waste of which the Japanese people were not aware. The Japanese live almost entirely on rice and sea food, but children need milk, and adults thrive on meat and protein. It seemed quite apparent to Rusch that the obvious move for Japan to make was to start raising dairy and beef cattle on the waste lands. So he and a few Japanese friends decided to see if it could be done, and at the same time to initiate an experiment in the democratic methods which Rusch had been describing. They induced the Japanese government to donate a piece of a mountain nobody wanted, Rusch's fellow officers raised some money, and the Kiyosato Educational Experiment began.

One might pause an instant and note the modest dimensions of the enterprise. Rusch particularly wanted to keep it that way. Shiny tractors and paved roads would impress American vistors, but would only discourage the proud Japanese, who would know they could not for years afford to create such luxuries without help. The whole point of Kiyosato was to create something which the Japanese could copy *without help*. It was to give them an idea, and with the idea a chance for pride and self-reliance and accomplishment—democracy in the only true sense. Kiyosato was to be an example which would furnish the people with an opportunity for self-development and justifiable pride—not a hand-out which would make them dependent, humiliate them, and in the end arouse their furious resentment, as has been the tragic lot of the American government's official programs in Asia. The fact that so few among American officialdom comprehend this simple and basic part which the desire for independence and human dignity plays in the hearts of the world's peoples is the real American weakness. This more than any other fact may finally destroy our position among the nations of the earth. Of this weakness Paul Rusch wanted no share. He had lived in Asia. He was one American who understood.

In Kiyosato almost everything was done by the people themselves. What equipment they were given was secondhand and inexpensive—an old bus and a bulldozer, a discarded dentist's chair and a used X-ray machine. They all worked, however. The experiment grew and prospered. People in the United States donated cattle. A farmer in Nebraska gave a prize bull. Soon in Kiyosato self-respect and a sense of personal accomplishment were in the very air. People joked and laughed about their difficulties. The farmers sang as they walked to the fields. Success is intoxicating, and success brought by one's own efforts, doubly so. When the experiment began, there were only a few animals, but now there are over two thousand cows peacefully grazing on the hitherto useless hills. Young men from all over Japan are flocking in to study the enterprise with a view to establishing similar success in their own areas. This was what Paul Rusch wanted. The bitter hills of Japan will be bitter no longer. The children of Japan will have meat and milk. Already, around Kiyosato, the children are taller, and they have better teeth and are in better health than their parents.

Perhaps most significant of all is the fact that the Communists have paid Kiyosato the tribute of opposing it at each step. They have fought it in every possible way. All their efforts, however, have been useless. Opposition to Kiyosato is not popular among the people of Japan, and the Communists know better than to press their opposition too far.

Young Dr. Tom Dooley has used in Laos the same approach Paul Rusch employed in Japan. Dooley established small, local hospitals and then turned them over to the people themselves, to be run under the direction of their own leaders. When saying good-by to Prince Phelserath of Laos, Dooley explained what he was doing and why he was doing it. The Prince replied emphatically, "Good!" The Prince went on to say that aid should not be given in such a way as to cause a people to become "dependent on the aider," and that the one true "aid" was the kind which automatically turned itself over to the people themselves.[2]

In Laos, which is a tropical country cruelly crippled by disease, and in Japan, where only 16 per cent of the land can be cultivated, such people as Tom Dooley and Paul Rusch generate a force which goes far beyond their immediate vicinities. There should be thousands of such men and women, not a mere handful. But the fact may be that much of the genius of these Americans has sprung from their peculiar type of voluntarism and their humility. Our foreign aid officials, who with staffs and limousines and servants move about the backward countries with apparently unlimited money and tell the people what is good for them, must surely represent one of the most insufferable outpourings of arrogance the world has ever witnessed. The American technician, on the other hand, develops solutions but does not impose them. He simply enables a new idea to come in and grow by its own vitality on native soil. Among the people self-respect is increased, instead of the reverse.

One may doubt if any technique other than this is practical. It is customary to say that if the gap between living standards of the underdeveloped nations and living standards in the West is not narrowed, there will be an explosion. The example most generally cited is India. But look for a moment at the actual problem India faces. If the entire accumulation of the United States agricultural surplus were, in a heroic effort at distribution, successfully moved to India and equitably distributed, it would relieve India's chronic starvation for less than one year.[3] Similarly, if all the United States food surplus for 1959 was successfully distributed throughout the globe, it would equal about two teacups of rice every seventeen days for each of the world's undernourished people. It is impossible to pretend that there can be any solution to world hunger by the patchwork of sporadically transporting supplies. The dimension of the problem is too large. The nations themselves must develop solutions, which may of course include regular import and acceptance of gifts. But the arrogant parody we have called "foreign aid" can never be the answer even under the best of circumstances. The solution must lie in the genius of each nation as it faces its own problems, and in the intelligent diffusion of advanced agricultural techniques —fertilizers, seed, and soil improvement—in freedom. This is the kind of aid we can give.

It is time that America asserted her own most native genius, common sense.

CHAPTER V

THE SOVIET ECONOMIC THREAT:
WHAT IS IT?

There is an old saying that there are three kinds of lies—lies, damn lies, and statistics. But there are actually four kinds of lies. The fourth kind of lie is the half-truth.

Early in 1959 I received from the State Department a booklet entitled *The Communist Economic Threat*. This booklet was sent to me in my capacity as a newspaper editor, and its purpose was to persuade me, and through me the public, that the Communists in the Kremlin were using "a new weapon, economic penetration. It could be," said the booklet, "the most dangerous of all weapons in the Communists' varied arsenal."

Then it went on to document what it termed the "immensity" of this Communist "economic warfare." "Since 1954," it stated, "the Soviet bloc countries have concluded agreements with eighteen of the less well developed countries outside the Soviet orbit which provide for the extension of an estimated $2,400,000,000 in intermediate and long term credits and grants for goods and services from the bloc."

Now that sounds indeed like rather formidable competition in foreign aid spending, doesn't it? But it is a half-truth, and when you get the other half, you see that it is a lie.

Here is the other half of that half-truth.

First, the United States has, during that same period, given away and loaned more than $24,000,000,000 to over sixty countries in the world. That is ten times the Soviet's "estimated" program. In foreign aid we are, therefore, doing ten times as much as the Soviets.

But that is only part of the other half of the truth. Most American aid is given away, while most of the Soviet aid is straight credits at rates of interest from 2 to 2½ per cent.

Furthermore, the "$2,400,000,000" Soviet credit program is figured at the official Soviet rate of exchange, which is four rubles to a dollar. But the hard fact is that the Soviet official rate is only a bad joke in world money markets. Its actual worth is a fraction of the official claim.[1]

The myth of the Soviet ruble is easily exploded. The Perrera Company in New York, which deals in foreign exchange, states that a dollar equals twenty-five to fifty rubles in real buying power, depending on the commodity. Also there are very few people in the international market for rubles. Let us show the maximum charity to the Soviet foreign aid program, however, and figure that twenty-four rubles will buy one dollar. What do we find then? We find that at twenty-four rubles to a dollar instead of the official four, we have to cut the dollar amount of the Soviet program down to one sixth of what is claimed. So the $2,400,000,000 Soviet program becomes only $400,000,000. This means that the Soviet Union actually has a program of spending $100,000,000 a year in gifts and loans. So now, after revealing a little more of the other half of the truth, the Soviet "economic threat" is sixty times less in dollars than our foreign aid program!

We must not stop here. The State Department booklet says "only about thirty-eight per cent of the credits [for those eighteen countries] have been drawn." Therefore, the program of the Kremlin, estimated at $2,400,000,000 and found to be only $400,000,000 in actual dollars, in reality has provided only 38 per cent of that amount or $152,000,000 in four years. So what do we find now? We find that the "economic threat" of the Soviet Union has diminished to $38,000,000 a year, or an infinitesimal six one hundredths of our own program. That, fellow Americans, is peanuts, as anyone who reads the astronomical figures of our budget must know. And yet we are implored to increase our already crippling expenses for foreign aid to meet this puny threat!

Furthermore, to compare this expenditure of the Soviet Union to our own foreign spending *in any regard* is grotesque. Private American charitable institutions *donate* approximately $500,000,000 every year to foreign countries. American tourists *alone* spend over $2,000,-000,000 a year in foreign lands. If the United States government abolished its entire foreign aid program, tourists and private charities would still be pouring more dollars into foreign countries *each year* than the Soviet government claims to spend in four! In fact, American tourists and American charitable agencies spend sixty-six times as much as the Soviet Union, without costing the United States taxpayer a cent. In addition, there are billions of dollars invested in foreign countries by American private industry and business which must also be added to the total of non-government "foreign aid" from the United States.

In the last ten years, almost $300,000,000,000 (yes, that is billions) has been sent abroad by the United States. Purchases of foreign goods have amounted to $190,000,000,000. Private donations to religious and charitable organizations have totalled $7,000,000,000. Private investments in foreign lands have come to $27,-000,000,000. The rest, $75,000,000,000 to $80,000,000,000 has been government gifts and loans. All of the private money sent abroad has been used to stimulate business, provide new equipment, take care of the destitute and rebuild foreign economies, in contrast to what we have seen often happened to our mishandled government-to-government aid.

The total foreign trade done by the Soviet Union in 1957 was 33,000,000,000 rubles. It is not appreciably more today. Translated into real dollars at the generous figure of twenty-four rubles to a dollar, that would be a total Soviet trade of $1,387,000,000. But 24,500,000,000 rubles-worth of this trade is entirely inside the Soviet bloc! Trade with non-Communist nations was only 7,000,000,000 rubles a year or $290,000,000. That is less than France spends in Africa every year. Free world trade with Asia and Africa alone is $23,000,000,000 a year or ninety-two times as much as total Soviet trade with the entire free world![2]

The entire Soviet foreign trade, both inside and outside the Communist bloc was 3.6 per cent of world exports and 3⅓ per cent of world imports. Even if that were doubled in the next ten years, an unlikely prospect, it would still be relatively tiny. Certainly it is no threat to free world trade anywhere, except inside the Soviet bloc, where free world trade cannot penetrate anyhow.

So what do we find when we get the whole other side of the half-truth about Communist "economic warfare"? *We find that effectively there is no such thing.* We find that American private investment, charitable giving, and tourists are doing one hundred times more than the Soviet Union is doing, or can do in any foreseeable future, in providing economic strength for foreign countries. We find that Americans are being lied to about the nature of the Soviet threat. We find that half-truths, which are more dangerous than lies because they are more easily believed, are being used to frighten the public into maintaining the security and power of the people whose private interests are entrenched in the foreign aid program. These people's jobs depend on the program. Naturally they want to see it grow. It would be very hard to make them admit that they are, in fact, simply exploiting their fellow-citizens.

When Lincoln said, "You can fool some of the people all of the time, and all of the people some of the time, but you can't fool all of the people all of the time," maybe in that era he was right. But about foreign aid it does seem that in our day the State Department publicity men have been doing a pretty good job of fooling all of the people all of the time.

Back in December, 1958, I wrote an editorial called "Foreign Aid for Communists." From the Library of Congress I had received a breakdown of the expenditures of the United States government in countries under Communist control. What struck me most about this breakdown was the large sums which had been siphoned off to Communist countries since 1955. For instance, in 1955 the United States provided $2,374,000 to Communist Czechoslovakia. Between 1954 and 1958 we sent $17,-339,000 to Communist Germany. In 1955 we sent $3,-496,000 to Communist Hungary. But even worse, in 1957, after the tragic end of the Hungarian revolt against Communism, we sent $10,166,000 to Communist Hungary—for what purpose?—as a reward for the slaughter of their countrymen?

Between July and December of 1957 we sent Communist Poland $49,890,000. More went there in 1958. And as we have seen, our old friend Tito, the dictator of

Yugoslavia, has received almost $1,000,000,000 since 1946 with $402,000,000 of it being sent between 1955 and 1958. Yugoslavia got, in real dollars, about $27,000,000 from the Soviet Union in the same period.

The officials of the International Cooperation Administration became excited when the editorial prepared from this Library of Congress material was printed in the *Congressional Record*, and pointed questions were asked about aid to Communist countries. During the 1959 session of Congress, a nine-page "rebuttal" was circulated among members of the House and Senate Foreign Relations Committees. Stress was laid on the fact that in many cases, Albania's for instance, all American aid was given in 1946 and 1947, right after the war when the Communists were still "our allies." It was also pointed out that in the other cases, the bulk of the United States aid was sent to Communist bloc nations in 1946 and 1947. This does not alter the fact that we gave them the money. We also gave about $500,000,000 directly to the Soviet Union at the same time. What this fact actually indicates is the fatal and now almost incredible blindness in this country, which did not realize until 1948 that the Soviet Union was dangerous to our national survival.

ICA officials also pointed out that at the time aid was given to Czechoslovakia—in 1946, for instance—that country was not under Communist domination. Soviet troops occupied Czechoslovakia, and the argument for foreign aid is that it is successful in keeping free countries out of the Soviet orbit. Did the $20,000,000 we gave to Albania keep her out of Communism's grip? Did the $138,000,000 we gave to Czechoslovakia prevent the murder of Jan Masaryk or prevent Communism from seizing the country? Did our aid make Poland free from Communism in 1947? Let's not be silly.

All told, we have provided more than $2,000,000,000 in American money to the Soviet bloc since 1946. That is more than enough to finance the entire Soviet "economic offensive" against the free world.

ICA officials say that most of this money went to help "the people," not the governments of these countries. That is simply nonsense. Does it help the people of East Germany or Hungary or Poland when we keep their government financially strong? Every expenditure we undertake within those countries relieves their governments of the necessity of spending money they might otherwise have had to spend. It should be obvious that by bailing out Tito year after year from Communist-made economic and social perils, we have strengthened the continuance of his tyranny. We have actually sided with him against the people of Yugoslavia. Over and over again our government-to-government system of aid causes us to assist dictators in further crushing and exploiting some of the most subjugated peoples of the globe. Our absurd and stupid policies obscure our national image in the eyes of other nations everywhere. And, most dangerously of all, they strengthen the enemy and weaken our own power to survive. In this period our gold reserves are drained. Our economists point with anxiety to our heavy taxation which makes it difficult for America to find the capital necessary to expand our economy to the degree necessary to absorb the post-war population as it comes on the labor market. Our economic vitality is endangered by crushing taxation. Why? So we can send $80,000,000 to Laos in time for the Communists to win another election?

CHAPTER VI

TO COMBAT SLAVERY:
WAGE FREEDOM

Where I live in Indiana the favorite sport of young and old is basketball. For a Hoosier, excitement reaches a peak during the high-school basketball season. Coaches vie in creating new offensives and special plays. No matter how varied these stratagems appear, however, all are designed for a single purpose—to defeat the other teams and win the state championship. Each player and every coach knows there is only one objective, to play as hard as possible—in short, to win.

Never in Indiana was there such a team as the one which takes the floor each week in international diplomacy. For the sake of the metaphor let's call it the Blue Team. Here it is—a group composed of stars from half-a-dozen or more communities. It has four coaches and scores of potential players. But its main objective is only to hold down the score of the enemy, not to outscore him.

Its only strategy is to skirmish and stall. Its only plan is to outwait, not outwit.

The opposing team, the Red Team, counters this strategy with a full court press, driving, shooting, faking, always seeking to score, always planning to win.

Now in Indiana, if any coach handled his team the way the Blue Team's coaches do, he would be fired as fast as possible. But in the grotesque field house of international diplomacy, the same Blue coaches stay on and on, using the same mediocre and uncooperative players and losing game after game to the ruthlessly organizational Reds. Is not the conduct of American foreign policy ridiculous? Should not the objective of any intelligent foreign policy be to win for your country against your enemy? Is it not obvious that one coach who has one strategy and uses the best team he has, will do a better job than four coaches who are jealous of each other, and who all demand that their players play in every game regardless of ability? Will it not always be true that the best team, not the most popular players, will win?

Suppose we make the comparison more concrete. Let us say that the five players on each of the diplomatic teams engaged in the conflict of liberty versus Communism are: 1. Forward—diplomacy, 2. Guard—economic power, 3. Forward—propaganda, 4. Guard—military power, and 5. Center—strategy (the playmaker). The coaches train the teams and work out the plays.

The Reds in the Soviet Union have one coach, and all players are picked for their ability. The plan is to keep the opponent off balance. Instructions are to outwit, out-shoot and outthink the enemy, and to break the rules of the game whenever profitable.

The Blues of the NATO powers have at least four coaches—United States, Britain, France, and West Germany. Each has his own special plan. The head coach, the United States, often finds the allied players trying plays he never told them to use, passing off when they should shoot, shooting when they should have passed off, and breaking up the teamwork. Also he has been committed by the Council of Coaches to play a defensive game in order to keep from getting too rough for the allied players. He has to devise a stall, ways to hold the ball as long as possible, never shoot until the opponents have been maneuvered out of range, and above all, never anger the Reds by seeming to be trying to win. At the same time, however, he must keep the Reds from winning.

Nobody can win that way!

Napoleon once said, "Give me a coalition to fight against." That is because he knew that division, jealousy, disputes over strategy and tactics, national jealousies, and national interests keep an enemy divided so that his forces can be kept off balance by sudden strikes here and there, by swift maneuver always directed from a single authority.

Of course, we know that foreign policy is not a game. Naturally, we understand that it is necessary for the United States to consult our allies. But it is also true that on those many occasions when the interests and demands of our allies weaken our effectiveness in our conflict with the Reds, we must find ways to be ready to put our own team directly onto the field. Our own diplomacy, strategy, propaganda, and economic and military power must be allowed to function in our defense. We cannot afford to be crippled and inefficient in today's dangerous game of international domination. For the price of defeat is not only loss of our own lives and liberty but the existence of the entire free world.

What must Americans do to protect the interests of the people of the United States and to defeat the Communist strategy for world conquest? The first step is squarely to face the fact that we are already in a war with the Communists. We have been in that war ever since international Communism established its first base in Soviet Russia. This is a fact of which they were always aware, even when we were not; and all their actions are based on it. For us not to understand it has been sheer folly.

The next step we must take is to resolve firmly to *win* the war we are in. We must win it without allowing the cold war, which depends on economic, political, strategic, and propaganda forces, to turn into a military war. We have to act as though our diplomats, our economic strength, our political skill were actually front line soldiers in a new kind of struggle. It is worldwide in scope and it is a struggle to the death. Either liberty and national independence or Communism and national extinction will win.

Once we recognize the kind of war we are in, and resolve to win it, we will win it. But we have to realize the truth about Soviet Communism, to understand its utterly ruthless and dangerous nature, and to face the facts about this decisive contest, which if we lose by seeking only to defend ourselves from attack, and by allowing ourselves to be crippled by the conflicting interests of our allies, we will lose everything. This America which has been one of the wonders of the world will vanish forever.

Winston Churchill wrote in 1939, when the full degree of Hitler's threat was understood by only a few in Britain, "If you will not fight for the right when you can easily win without bloodshed; if you will not fight when your victory will be sure and not too costly; you may come to the moment when you will have to fight with all the odds against you and only a precarious chance of survival."[1] England would not fight when Hitler could have been toppled with relative ease. She did not realize that even in those earlier days she was fighting for her life. Therefore, she had to fight after she had allowed Hitler's Germany to grow to almost fatal power. She had to fight "with all the odds against her"—to be saved only by the might of the United States. And who is there now, to save us?

America under John Foster Dulles fought the Communist advance, but the techniques were defensive. Dulles sought to hold what the free world still had, believing that by stopping the Communist advance, America could keep her liberty, while waiting for the Soviet Union to fall from within.

Defense does not win victories. Only offense brings victory.

How do we seize the offensive against the Soviet thrust? First we must free our minds from the cunningly focused Soviet propaganda which claims that either the West must negotiate with the Soviet Union or there will be atomic war. There are prominent spokesmen in the West who have believed in this naive pair of alternatives: "Either we wage peace by argument or we wage war to the general ruin."[2] This is a wholly unfounded pattern of either-or. Naturally the Communists are pleased when we believe it. They, of course, do *not* believe it, as they constantly prove. For while *we* negotiate, *they* act. They overwhelm part of a country or subvert a government or "rectify" a border, or engage in some other definite action. This is neither hot war nor cold war, but a third way to achieve their objectives: they are *waging Communism.* We could also have a third way, if we will only take heart. We should *wage freedom.*

To wage freedom requires that we recognize as our objective the roll-back of Communism from one country after another, the use of our political, strategic, economic, diplomatic, and propaganda power to win the world for liberty, just as our enemy has been capturing it for Communism. Does not a feeling of warmth and strength surge in us as we consider even the possibility of waging freedom? Is it not altogether alien to everything that America is for us to go on abandoning to slavery people after people despite their pleas for help? That warmth which surges in you—does it not flow from our deepest national vitality, our true historic self?

Those who advocate quiet surrender to the Russian global seizures are as quick to quote Washington's speech in order to keep us from acting today, as they were to sneer at it as being out of date when it was being quoted in the thirties in an effort to restrain us from alliance with the Soviet Union because of our antipathy to Hitler. It is high time that someone considered what Washington's speech really meant. From the beginning, this speech has been regarded as a basic expression of what America is. The conditions it describes have come to represent in our consciousness a fundamental aspect of our national identity. They also describe a primary image of ourselves which grew in the consciousness of the world. In discussing this speech, therefore, we are not merely paying tribute to eloquent words spoken by a single historical figure, but examining motive-springs of international action—our own actions toward the world, and the world's action toward us. So what was Washington actually talking about?

It is clear that he was talking about two things which are in opposition; the first was principle and the second was prejudice. He enjoined us above all things to adhere to principle, pleading in his key phrase that we "observe faith and justice toward all nations." On the other hand, he warned us against prejudice, particularly against the power of prejudice to obscure common sense and even the sense of self-preservation. "Inveterate antipathies against particular nations and passionate attachments for others" can make a nation "slave" to "animosity" or "affection," either of which is sufficient "to lead it astray from its duty and its interest." These last ten words hold the heart of the matter. We are to avoid prejudice in order to pursue an all important purpose. That twofold purpose is "duty and interest." Nothing must blind us to these. Interest refers to our self-preservation as a nation. Duty refers back to the principles of "good faith and justice."

In the 1930s, antipathy to the fascists and attachment to those called anti-fascist blinded us to the Soviet threat to our own self-preservation and the threat to whatever faith and justice still existed in the world. Today it is naive to say that our attitude is one of mere antipathy or attachment. Naturally we do have antipathies to the Soviet Union—we do not, for instance, like some of the methods used by their secret police. We also must admit attachments to other nations—we profoundly pity, for example, Hungary. But few persons today claim, in our situation as it has now developed, our actions are or should be based on attachment and antipathy. True, our aversion to Russian methods and our pity for Hungary, for example, exist in our present national character, but they are the outer layer. The core of our character, the very center of our identity, now and always, is our existence as a nation. If we cease to exist, all other matters become for us entirely academic.

To wage freedom does not mean to plunge into atomic war. To wage freedom is a third way, which lies between hot war and cold war. It may mean, for example, to give India, if she wishes it, unilateral assistance in her border dispute with China. It would certainly mean, in many areas, policies of far greater courage and initiative than we have shown in the past. It also means having in reserve a total military striking power so alert and formidable that the Soviet Union will not dare risk a full military collision in hope of catching us napping. "Napping" is a state we can never afford to be in.

When we put victory first and peace second we are doing nothing revolutionary. We are merely being faithful to our authentic character. Most cities and towns have somewhere a plaque or a statue to Patrick Henry. Most of us know essentially what he said. But nearly all would be astonished at how freshly minted and moving his words sound in our own crisis. If we change the terms which he applied to the men and circumstances of that time, and substitute for them the names which apply to men and circumstances of today, we can scarcely believe that his speech is not newly spoken for us, his countrymen who live in 1960. Listen:[3]

"I entertain opinions of a character exactly opposite to the opinions of our top foreign policymakers. I shall speak forth my sentiments freely and without reserve.

This is no time for ceremony. The question before us all is one of awful moment to this country. For my part, I consider it as nothing less than a question of freedom and slavery.

"It is natural for man to indulge in the illusions of hope. We are apt to shut our eyes against a painful truth, and listen to the song of the siren, till she transforms us into beasts. Is this the part of wise men, engaged in a great and arduous struggle for liberty? Are we disposed to be of the number of those who, having eyes, see not, and having ears, hear not the things which so nearly concern their temporal salvation? For my part, whatever anguish of spirit it may cost, I am willing to know the whole truth; to know the worst, and to provide for it.

"We have but one lamp by which our feet are guided; and that is the lamp of experience. We know of no way of judging the future, but by the past. And judging by the past, I wish to know what there has been in the conduct of the Soviet government in the last forty years to justify the hopes expressed by our policymakers concerning conferences with the Communists. Is it that insidious smile with which N. S. Khrushchev received our proposal for negotiations? We should not trust Khrushchev's smile, for it will prove a snare. We should ask ourselves how the latest Moscow smiles comport with the Soviet war preparations which cover the waters and darken the land. Are the huge and ever increasing Soviet armed forces necessary to a work of love and reconciliation? Have we shown ourselves so unwilling to be recon-

ciled, that force must be called in to win back our love?
Let us not deceive ourselves. The Communist arms are
the implements of war and subjugation; the last arguments to which tyrants resort. What is the meaning of
the Soviet martial array, if its purpose be not to force
America into submission? Can there be any other possible motives for it? Has Soviet Russia any enemy in the
world to call for this accumulation of arms? No, she has
not. The Soviet arms are meant for us; they can be meant
for no other.

"And what have we to oppose them? Shall we try argument? We have been trying that for the last fifteen years.
Have we anything new to offer on the subject? Nothing.
We have held the subject up in every light in which it is
capable, but it has all been in vain. What terms will we
find which have not already been exhausted? Let us not
deceive ourselves any longer. We have done everything
that could be done to avert the present crisis. We have
petitioned; we have remonstrated; we have supplicated;
we have prostrated ourselves before the tyrannical men
in Moscow. Our petitions have been slighted; our remonstrances have produced additional violence and in-
sults; our supplications have been disregarded; and we
have been spurned with contempt from the foot of the
Red throne in the Kremlin.

"In vain after these things may we indulge the hope
of peace and reconciliation. There is no longer any room
for such hope. If we wish to be free; if we mean to preserve inviolate those inestimable privileges for which we

have been so long contending; if we mean not basely to abandon the noble struggle in which we have been so long engaged, we must be prepared to resist the Soviet onslaught, if necessary by force. To repeat—we must be prepared to resist the Soviet onslaught, if necessary by force.

"It is argued that we may be unable to cope with so formidable an adversary as Soviet Russia. But when shall we be stronger? Will it be next week or the next year? Would it be when we are totally disarmed and when Red guards are stationed in all American cities? Shall we gather strength by irresolution and inaction? Shall we acquire the means of effective resistance by lying supinely on our backs, and hugging the delusive phantom of hope, until our Communist enemies shall have bound us hand and foot?

"We are not weak, if we make proper use of the means which God has placed in our power. One hundred and seventy million Americans, united in the holy cause of liberty, and representing such a country as that which we possess, are invincible by any force which our Communist enemies can send against us. Besides, we are not in this struggle alone. There is a just God who presides over the destinies of nations and who will raise friends to come on our side. The struggle ahead is not for the strong alone. It is for the vigilant, the active, the brave. Besides, we have no choice. If we were base enough to desire it, it is now too late to retire from the contest.

There is no retreat but in submission and slavery. The Communists have forged our chains. Their clanking may be heard in the mountains of Tibet or on the plains of Hungary or in the city of East Berlin.

"Diplomats in Geneva may cry peace, peace, but there is no peace. The cold war has long since begun, and the hot war is inevitable unless we win the cold war. If we lose the political struggle with the Soviets, the next gale that sweeps from the Communist East may well bring to our ears the clash of resounding arms. Our brethren are already in the field—in Tibet, in Red China, in enslaved East Europe, and even inside Russia herself. Why stand we here idle? What is it that the appeasers among us wish? What would they have? If life is so dear, peace so sweet, as to be purchased at the price of chains and slavery? Forbid it, Almighty God! I know not what course others may take; but as for me, give me liberty, or give me death!"

Portions of this speech have been declaimed in so many schoolrooms, spoken on so many fourths of July, used to ornament so many political speeches. But the very frequency with which they have been engraved on our national consciousness may seem to many of us to weaken them. They may seem hackneyed, and it is easy to overlook how deeply they are part of us. But it is absolutely impossible to make them not be part of us, to push them aside, contradict them, or wipe them out. Of all the free people left on the globe, there is not one to whom loss of freedom would be more agonizing than to Americans.

Therefore how shall we go about preserving the liberty whose loss is indeed worse than death?

As a first step let us consider the problem of winning the cold war without starting a hot one. Let us take as an example the 1959 Geneva Conference of Foreign Ministers. What happeneed there?

The Soviets demanded that the Allied powers get out of Berlin and recognize the authority of East Germany. They demanded that we hold a summit conference to bring this about. We refused. But we agreed to discuss the problem saying that we would not relinquish our rights in Berlin.

The Soviet Union was making new demands, abrogating its own past agreements with us on Berlin and taking the diplomatic offensive to force us to go to the summit, the chief aim of which, even if it did not win new concessions from the Allies, was to bolster Khrushchev's standing in his own country and throughout the world.

We simply went on the defensive and stood our ground. But suppose we had deliberately taken the offensive? Certainly we had been given ample opportunities. Suppose we had said to Khrushchev: "We will go to the summit under these conditions: 1. First you must fulfill the agreement you made with us at the last summit conference: namely, that the reunification of Germany by means of free elections shall be carried out in conformity with the national interests of the German people and the interests of European security. 2. Next you must honor your previous agreements to permit free elections in Hungary, Poland, Czechoslovakia, Rumania, Bulgaria, Albania. 3. We also demand that you fulfill the treaty of recognition of 1933, whereby you agreed to stop sending financial and other aid to the American Communist Party and to end all support for American Communists."

Then we would add a clear statement of principle: namely, that it is the objective of American foreign policy to give every possible aid short of war to all people seeking freedom and national independence, even in the Soviet Union, and that it is our intention to bring about, by any and all peaceful means, the downfall of the Communist system because it enslaves the individual and destroys national independence.

At the same time we might propose that American troops will withdraw from Europe, if the Soviets withdraw troops from all of Eastern Europe, including Latvia, Lithuania, and Esthonia under United Nations supervision, and that token United Nations troops will be stationed in these countries until they have established governments freely chosen by the people.

Now if we had taken such a position, would the Soviet Union have started war against us? On what pretext? We would only have been asking them to fulfill their solemn obligations under treaties and agreements they had already made. We would only have been declaring what they declare when they say, that they will "bury us." We are simply stating that we intend to win the cold war, as they have stated that they intend to do.

The Soviet leaders will not start a war against the United States unless they are fully convinced that they can win it. Communist strategists say themselves that they do not believe in going to war until victory is assured, until the United States is cut off from all allies in Europe and Asia and surrounded by Communist nations. The Communists employ war only as a means to Communist domination. They will never go to war over words or threats or pieces of property, as was proved when they drew back from Quemoy and Matsu, when they pulled out of Iran before a determined American military stand, as was proved in Greece when American troops went in under General Van Fleet, as was proved when American troops landed, however unwisely, in Lebanon in the face of Soviet threats.

To mount a skillful, unrelenting offensive of this sort the United States must enjoy autonomy of action. She must, when necessary, ignore the desires and fears of her allies. We must make it plain to the British and French and West Germans that it is our power that protects them from Soviet domination, and that it is therefore our responsibility to use that power as we know it must be used in order to defeat the Communist attempt to dominate the world. If they do not agree, we can simply say that they may go their own way if they wish, alone. It is not likely that they will, but in any case American policy must be based on the belief that every nation has a right to national independence, and every citizen the right to be governed by a government of his own choice. America must hold true to this central idea, which has been and is the moral and historical position of her people and government since the founding of the Republic.

CHAPTER VII

"THE GREATEST TYRANNY
HAS SMALL BEGINNINGS"

In the harbor of the Turkish port of Smyrna in 1853 the American warsloop "Saint Louis" swung into firing position, its guns aimed at the brig "Huzar," a warship of the Royal Austrian government. Captain Duncan Nathaniel Ingraham had just issued an ultimatum to the Austrian commander: "Surrender Martin Koszta, or I will begin to fire." Just before the deadline, a boat was lowered from the "Huzar," and Martin Koszta was surrendered to the Americans.[1]

Martin Koszta was not yet a full citizen of the United States, but he had taken out his first citizenship papers. Therefore, in the eyes of the American government he was no longer an Austrian citizen, subject to the conscription laws of the Austrian Empire. Nevertheless, he had been seized by the Austrian navy in Smyrna and put aboard the "Huzar" to be taken in chains back to Austria which claimed him as a citizen. When his kidnapping was discovered, the American minister in Constantinople immediately issued orders to Captain Ingraham to demand his release, and to use force if necessary. Ingraham told the commander of the "Huzar" that he knew the intention was to smuggle Koszta out to Trieste. Therefore he put a time limit on the surrender, saying he would open fire if Koszta was not immediately turned over.

When this episode was made known to the Austrian government, Baron Hulsemann, Austrian chargé d'affaires in Washington, sent a formal note to Secretary of State William Learned Marcy demanding that the United States "disavow" Ingraham's action, "tender to Austria a satisfaction proportionate to the magnitude of the outrage," and extradite Koszta forthwith.

Marcy replied on behalf of the United States in the now famous "Hulsemann Letter." "Whenever by the law of nations an individual becomes clothed with the national character . . . he can claim the protection of this government, and it may respond to that claim without being obliged to explain its conduct to any foreign power; for it is its duty to make its nationality respected by other nations and respectable in every quarter of the globe."

According to the 1909 edition of *Nelson's Encyclopaedia*, "The affair established a precedent since followed in cases resembling it by the United States government."

Will it be followed in 1960? Was it followed in the

1950s? Could any encyclopedia today write what it was still possible to write as short a time ago as 1909?

In 1958, nine United States soldiers were kidnapped by Communist Germany, nine United States airmen were shot down over Armenia, forty-seven American civilians, sailors, and marines were kidnapped by Castro forces in Cuba. About that same time John Noble, an American who had been imprisoned without cause in a Soviet slave labor camp, was quoted in an interview as saying, "Every day the Russians taunted us, 'If you had a government in America, they'd get you out.' "[2]

The American government of the 1940s and 1950s has managed to find only weak verbal protests to counter almost incessant humiliations, kidnappings, imprisonments, and deaths of its citizens abroad. We actually paid ransom to one Communist government, which had shot down American fliers behind the iron curtain. There are four hundred and fifty American prisoners of war known to be held by Red China in violation of the Korean armistice. These men were serving their country. Now they rot in Communist jails. The government of the United States, which once risked war with one of the most powerful empires in Europe when only a fledgling itself, can barely summon up the courage to hold "conferences."

In 1853 Americans made clear to the world their unshakable belief in the value of the individual human being, they established the firm precedent that the rights of the individual must be protected at all costs, and that

Americans in every quarter of the globe could, in Secretary of State Marcy's words, claim "the protection of this government."

Could anyone contend that Bill Oatis[3] and Robert Vogeler,[4] when imprisoned in Eastern Europe by Communist governments, received the protection of their own government? Is it true in any part of the world today that "the Constitution follows the flag"? We now permit foreign courts to try and sentence American soldiers. We have signed a treaty to that effect, although our drafted men are not abroad of their own free will, but have been sent to protect the nations where they are stationed. These nations have judicial processes entirely different from ours. To say that their justice is more primitive is an understatement. Recently in Turkey arrested American soldiers were submitted to the bastinado.[5]

The United States was founded on the principle that all men are endowed by their Creator with certain unalienable rights. It has been the historic character of America to give every citizen the protection of the Constitution and the law wherever he may be. Every American is a free man, protected in his freedom by the government he has chosen. We risked war with Austria over a lone Hungarian immigrant, who had only declared his intention of becoming an American citizen. We provoked war with Great Britain in 1812, when the British government began kidnapping Americans from American sailing vessels. In both cases our adversaries were far more powerful than we.

91

But today, when we are immeasurably the most powerful single nation in the world, we apparently do not dare even raise the threat of embargo to protect American citizens in foreign countries. Can there be any possible doubt of the contempt felt for us by the alertly watching peoples, aware as they are of the struggle to the death between us and our enemy? Which side will waverers be most apt to choose? Every battle in the minds of the watching peoples is actually a front-line conflict. Our enemy knows this and creates many situations deliberately. The conclusions of the onlooking world are made as easy as possible.

Have we lost our determination to protect the individual and his rights? Is the individual, the free American, no longer entitled to the protection Martin Koszta received? Apparently not. If Americans are willing to abandon their fellow-citizens to the tyranny and brutality of other governments for the sake of "peace" or "security," then how far can we be from being willing to abandon immemorial rights to life and liberty in our own country?

Hitler wrote, "To the Christian doctrine of the infinite significance of the individual human soul, I oppose with icy clarity the saving doctrine of the nothingness and insignificance of the human being."

Karl Marx wrote, "The democratic concept of man is false because it is Christian. The democratic concept holds that each man is a sovereign being. This is the illusion, the dream, the postulate of Christianity." It is also the central and fundamental principle of the United States. Or it was.

On the other hand, the Declaration of Independence says of the right to life, liberty, and the pursuit of happiness that "to secure these rights governments are instituted by men." It is the duty of every United States government to secure the rights of every United States citizen no matter what the cost, no matter what the risk. America was able to reach its present power because America put its principles first and was willing to dismiss the cost—"Millions for defense, not one cent for tribute" —and to ignore the risks—"Damn the torpedoes, full speed ahead." Now that we stand on our pinnacle of power are we to abandon the means which created it? Of such folly is compounded the death of nations.

It is certainly strange to see an American president accepting an invitation to go to Russia, whose government ordered the deaths of nine Americans without apology or indemnity. Even more peculiar is the invitation to Khrushchev to visit this country. Surely America is in a strange frame of mind! Some of our largest and most prominent church organizations propose that we recognize and trade with Communist China, the country which in violation of solemn agreement with us, still holds in prison four hundred and fifty of our citizens.

What incredible treachery it is to these men when our leaders go to Moscow to visit or "confer" with the overlords of the Kremlin! What a monstrous undermining of all principles of justice and good faith when Soviet leaders are entertained in the United States by private citizens and public officials, and the Soviet state press sees to it that Khrushchev, Mikoyan, Koslov, and the rest are shown surrounded by smiling groups of Americans in news photographs reproduced throughout the captive nations to prove to them that America has abandoned them! What does it mean in the eyes of the world when the top men of America and Great Britain go to Moscow and have to let themselves be insulted and degraded?

To the watching world it simply means that they are afraid not to go. Khrushchev, the dictator of a backward and brutal tyranny, has become a Roman emperor in the eyes of the world today. In the shadowy recesses of racial memory he is Tiberius, he is Nero, calling in neighboring kings to be exhibited to the crowds and prove he is master of the globe. In the historic memory of peoples, images centuries-old are stirred by these craven journeys to Moscow. The leaders of the free world walk in the shadows of ancient Asiatic and European embassies, trekking across the Russian plains to the abode of the Khans to grovel and beg for mercy from the Mongol tribes threatening to sweep across Europe with their murderous hordes. But Khrushchev is no Genghis Khan. The comparison of the power of Khrushchev with the power of Genghis Khan is ludicrous. Why do we allow the evocation of these fantasies? The United States has power to destroy the Soviet Union. Our nation is the most powerful in the world. But power, without the will to use it when necessary, is useless. The British and French discovered this when they faced a daring and rearming Hitler across the Rhine—and ended with appeasement at Munich and war. The Romans, centuries before them, discovered this when their great and glittering empire was assaulted by the barbarian tribes from the north who coveted their riches. The Babylonians, with their brilliant but decadent civilization, had the same experience before the onslaught of the more primitive Assyrians.

The Communists in the Soviet Union are openly bent on the destruction of free Europe and the United States. They have told us what they plan to do, as repeatedly as Hitler told his neighbors what he intended to do to them. Yet while we still have the power to resist and defeat them, while we have the strength to protect our liberties and secure ourselves against these terrors, we receive with honor and hospitality the visiting dignitaries of the Soviet Union, the suave and cunning Mikoyan, murderer of thousands of Hungarians, and Khrushchev himself, a creature whose brutality is legendary. The British Prime Minister went on his pilgrimage to Moscow, where he was insulted and forced to listen to harangues reviling British and American leaders. And still some of our legislators in Washington entertain thoughts of accepting Russian terms for whatever "conferences" they demand, calling this craven posture "flexibility." There can be no flexibility when compromise and surrender to the enemy means tyranny and slavery both for us and for the world.

It is better to die on your feet than to live on your belly.

It would be better for the United States to revive its old revolutionary slogan, "Don't Tread On Me," and face annihilation, than thus meanly give way and surrender a little at a time, our pride, the liberties of our friends, our treasure, and finally our independence as a nation. The stark alternatives of liberty or death are not yet before us, but if they were, can there be any doubt as to which is the one right choice?

It is a curious fact that the people who most lack the courage to endure the alternatives of war or loss of liberty should they actually come, are precisely the people most easily terrified into believing that they have in fact arrived. This fear is ridiculous. Russia wants atomic war even less than we. As I will prove in the next chapter, America's striking power is immeasurably greater than the striking power of the Soviet Union. Our strategic position is better. The historic plea of the coward for peace at any price cannot in this present context have even the shabby excuse of claiming necessity.

If we suffer a continuation of the ineptitude which has held American policy in its grip like some deathly paralysis, then we may indeed soon face alternatives of slavery or death. But the firm courage to face them if they do come is the best possible safeguard against their coming. The cowardly attitude which refuses to face them, and at the same time whines that they are already here, is the best invitation to their speedy arrival. In the recent novel *Advise and Consent*, Alan Drury, who in his capacity as Washington newsman has long been an astute observer of the events and psychology on Capitol Hill, creates for purposes of satire his fictitious peace-mongering Senator, Fred Van Ackerman. Ackerman, in one effective scene, is shown addressing a hysterical rally of the partisans of COMFORT (Committee On Making Further Offers for a Russian Truce). Cries Van Ackerman, "I say I had rather crawl to Moscow than die under a bomb!" while the hysterical partisans of COMFORT cheer wildly. Drury knows, as any person of common sense must know, that the surest way to die under a bomb, to lose the conflict with Russia, to enter slavery for all time, is to undertake the operation of the Moscow Crawl. But the Moscow Crawl is a popular mode of American mentality right now.

Adherence to principle is the basis of character for nations as for individuals. A nation which was founded upon principles, has kept them through history, and then begins to lose them is in a sense no longer itself. There are still men of courage in the world who will take immense risks for principle. How are the American people and their government currently responding to problems of principle? A significant example is the recent case of Povl Bang-Jensen.

In January, 1958, Bang-Jensen, a Danish diplomat in the United Nations, was suspended from his post by Secretary General Dag Hammarskjold. Basically, Bang-Jensen's offense was that he had refused to surrender the names of eighty-one Hungarians who had testified before the United Nations special committee on Hungary.

The eighty-one men were Hungarians who had tried to overthrow the Communist government and had been forced to flee before Russian troops when Soviet intervention crushed the revolution. These men had relatives still in Hungary, and they had agreed to testify only after having been given a guarantee by Bang-Jensen that he would not reveal their names to anyone outside the committee. Hammarskjold demanded that the names be turned over to the United Nations Secretariat for its files. Bang-Jensen refused, saying that they might fall into the hands of Communist employees of the Secretariat, and also that he could not in honor break his solemn promise to the men who testified.

I wrote an editorial in the *Indianapolis Star* praising Bang-Jensen's stand. Not long afterwards I received a letter from Mr. Bang-Jensen thanking us for our support and requesting copies of the editorial, which he hoped might help rally public opinion to his side. I wrote him to ask if he would tell his story if we came to New York. He replied that he had been forbidden to give interviews to newspapermen, but that he would see us as individuals, provided we did not publish any interview with him.

Michael Padev, the *Star's* foreign editor and I went to New York. I talked to Bang-Jensen alone first for about two hours. Then Padev talked to him for about three hours more. From our separate talks, we emerged with the same conclusion: namely, that Bang-Jensen was being railroaded out of his job at the demand of the Soviet members of the United Nations, who knew that their propaganda offensive had been deeply damaged by the special report on Hungary, and who recognized the propaganda offensive as the front-line battle it was. In this battle, the United States was destined to abandon Bang-Jensen first to the loss of his career, then to the loss of his life.

We investigated the case against Bang-Jensen. We read the Gross report, named for Ernest A. Gross, former United States Assistant Secretary of State and a deputy representative of the United Nations, which said that Bang-Jensen violated United Nations rules by not turning over the names, and claimed that the names would be safe in the Secretariat. It also pointed to "aberrant behavior" and "gross misconduct" on Bang-Jensen's part. We read the entire sixty-page set of charges subsequently issued by Hammarskjold. Padev interviewed Andrew Cordier, an American who served as Hammarskjold's deputy and who appeared to be in charge of the specific offensive against Bang-Jensen. The more we learned, the more we became convinced that a Communist-inspired campaign was being waged against him. The purpose was to destroy Bang-Jensen and teach a lesson in terror, here on United States soil, to all who might have been tempted to trust American protection.

Bang-Jensen understood the stakes and realized his own danger. He was a married man (his wife was American) and he had five children. Nevertheless, he could not bring himself to surrender the eighty-one names.

There is reason now to suppose that he may have had more urgent grounds than any revealed at the time.[6] Evidence at present before a Senate committee indicates that when Bang-Jensen had once confided to some American United Nations officials the names of a number of iron curtain diplomats who wanted to break with Moscow and take refuge in the United States, the diplomats were suddenly recalled and possibly executed. We must remember that all the action in the Bang-Jensen case took place in the United States. Ernest Gross, Ralph Bunche, and particularly Andrew Cordier, all American citizens, were prominent in the affair. It seems next to impossible to assume that they were not actively hostile to him, believing him to be a danger to what they saw as the necessity to cooperate with the Soviet Union and never to antagonize its delegates. Ralph Bunche, in a reply to a letter protesting the treatment of Bang-Jensen and asking for a review of charges, wrote, "For the good of the individual we do not make public the nature of such charges and of personnel actions, which are purely internal matters."[7]

Bang-Jensen, of course, was fighting to have the charges made public so he could refute them. One cannot refute charges that no one knows. To be confronted by one's accusers is the historic right of free men. Bang-Jensen kept asking that documents on which charges were based, in the Gross report and in Hammarskjold's report, be given him so he could disprove the charges. He was convinced that if the real truth were told, he would be cleared of any blameworthy action. We discovered that Bang-Jensen had been offered $17,000 severance pay if he would resign quietly, but he refused and was finally fired and left without a job. Nevertheless, he continued to believe that with American support he would clear himself, while he realized that if he had resigned under fire his whole future would have lain under suspicion.

It became quite clear to us that the only real charge against Bang-Jensen in all the sixty pages of the Hammarskjold report was the single assertion that he failed, when ordered, to hand over the names of the Hungarians to whom he had given his personal promise not to reveal their identity. All other charges stemmed from that, and were obviously inserted as afterthoughts to strengthen the Secretariat's case. Most were based on acts which had occurred before he had refused to turn over the names and had insisted that the list be burned, for which he finally won permission and did himself, giving the paper to the flames with his own hands.

After pleading for months to be allowed to see the documents on which the Gross report was based and which he claimed would prove his innocence, Bang-Jensen issued his rebuttal. He stated that Hammarskjold refused to give him the due process of law to which he was entitled, that he could not see the documentary charges against him, that some of the documents which the Gross Committee claimed convicted him did not exist, and that the report on Hungary had, after it was written, been changed by someone to make it appear that the Soviets did not kidnap hundreds of Hungarians after smashing the revolt. He stated that two of the three men comprising the committee that first judged him were personal assistants to the man who signed the initial report against him. He said that Hammarskjold himself broke United Nations rules by setting up a committee which reached its conclusions before Bang-Jensen had a chance to testify in his own defense. He noted that some United Nations officials spread rumors to the effect that he was "a psychopathic troublemaker," mentally unbalanced. I might state here that while Padev and I are not psychiatrists, we are certainly as well qualified to judge Bang-Jensen's sanity as any of the United Nations officials, and to us he was obviously not only sane, but honorable and courageous to a degree almost unique in our time.

Bang-Jensen also charged that Charles Coates, an American member of the United Nations Disciplinary Committee, "had personal knowledge that the charges against me are false," and that when he had asked Coates' advice about accusations that the United Nations was being sabotaged from within by the Communists, Coates told him he was not entitled to do anything. "He even told me that in his opinion if the Secretary General had murdered his mother, he would not feel free to report it without the Secretary General's permission."

Then Bang-Jensen made a final and sensational statement. He said: "Many witnesses have been promised that nobody in the Secretariat but I would know their names. Several witnesses made this a condition for testifying. Two of them for very definite reasons which they specified, made it a condition that you [Secretary General Hammarskjold] in particular would not know their names" (a request for which one can readily supply the reason—the witnesses themselves believed that the secret of their identities would not be safe in the files of the Secretariat or in the hands of the Secretary).

Bang-Jensen's rebuttal was ignored by the Secretariat. It was ignored by virtually everyone involved.

What was the government of the United States, on which Bang-Jensen so pathetically counted, doing during all this time? The State Department knew the facts. The State Department also knew that Bang-Jensen had been a long-time friend and supporter of the United States and that he had been influential in working out the agreement between the United States and Denmark for our bases in Greenland during World War II, bases which significantly helped our war effort.

We at the *Star* had been carrying on a vigorous campaign with editorials and articles exposing the Bang-Jensen affair. Thousands of protests went from our readers and from people all over the country to the United States delegation at the United Nations, and to the State Department in Washington.

Ambassador Henry Cabot Lodge replied in a written statement that there was nothing he could do about the case, that he saw no reason why the names could not have been kept secret in the files of the Secretariat, and that the United States could not interfere in an "internal matter" in the United Nations. His deputy, James Wadsworth, issued a statement along the same lines, adding "I believe that Mr. Hammarskjold's letter shows that he was fully justified in dismissing Mr. Bang-Jensen." Anyway, he said, the list of names had now been burned, so the Hungarians were safe from any possible harm. Of course, the only reason the list had been burned was Bang-Jensen's insistence, which caused his dismissal.

In addition, the United States delegation circulated throughout the United States the whole Hammarskjold report, but refused to circulate with it the reply which Bang-Jensen had made to the charges against him.

As we repeatedly pointed out, the main charge against Bang-Jensen was his refusal to reveal the names of the Hungarian freedom fighters who testified before the committee. He had promised not to do so. Furthermore, he knew they would fall into the hands of Communist employees of the United Nations if they went into the Secretariat files. He had concrete evidence that this would happen.

On December 16, 1957, Dag Hammarskjold had announced that a Ceylonese United Nations employee had been dismissed for "misconduct." *He was charged with having delivered verbatim testimony from the Hungarian Committee to a member of the Soviet delegation.* He had been doing the very thing that Bang-Jensen, who had been in the United Nations for ten years, knew would be done if the names were made available to the United Nations Secretariat! And it is most interesting to note what happened to Dhanapala Samarasekara, the Ceylonese who was accused of stealing Hungarian Committee documents for the Soviet Union. He was allowed to resign his job "without prejudice" and given full terminal-leave pay. So successful is the terror inspired by the Soviet Union, that a United Nations employee dismissed on charges of stealing United Nations secrets for Russia, is rewarded by a comforting hand-out.

But when Bang-Jensen was summarily dismissed for trying to prevent Russians from stealing United Nations secrets, his natural protector, the United States, not only did nothing for him, but from fear of the enemy, joined in his harassment. Yet the Communist strategy was obvious. It was entirely clear that it was trying to avenge and discredit the United Nations report on Hungary by destroying Bang-Jensen.

The day after his dismissal was announced, Communist newspapers throughout Eastern Europe, with the swift unanimity they reserve for matters of importance, announced that this dismissal showed that the United Nations report on Hungary had been rigged against the Soviet Union by Bang-Jensen, and that the report was now publicly proved baseless.

Why did not Lodge, our ambassador, support Bang-Jensen's obviously true contention that a promise is made in honor, and that the lives of men and women still in Hungary depended on not revealing the names of those who testified? Why did not the State Department back up the Danish government in its support of this man, who put his own career on the block to protect the lives of people who had dared everything to fight Communist tyranny? Little Denmark, its press and politicians backing up its government, supported Bang-Jensen with money and diplomatic protest. But the powerful United States seemed paralyzed.

Individually, what persons in America came to Bang-Jensen's defense? Among the politicians, very few; and they could almost have been named in advance: Robert Morris, Barry Goldwater, William E. Jenner. Among private individuals were only a few newspapermen on such papers as the *Arizona Republic,* the *Brooklyn Tablet,* or our own *Indianapolis Star.* Most American politicians and most newspapers were silent. The press services carried little on this demonstration of Communist vengeance. The sacrifice of a career for honor and for the protection of helpless people left America unmoved.

Later, when Bang-Jensen's body, with a bullet hole in his temple and a twenty-five caliber automatic by his side, was found on a bridle path near his Long Island home, the press finally paid some attention. And in Washington Democratic Senator Thomas J. Dodd of Connecticut, a former FBI agent and acting chairman of a Senate Internal Security Subcommittee, pressed for an investigation, particularly to discover whether this death was indeed suicide or another murder at the hands of Communist agents. A rural road, a Washington hotel—

any characteristically American setting is valuable as a lesson to would-be refugees from, or fighters of Communism; and in the United States at present the suspected but unpublicized murders of this type are many. But whether Bang-Jensen in despair killed himself, or whether another hand held the gun, makes little difference. It was murder either way. And whatever the result of the investigation, and whatever the press and public reaction now, it is too late for the man of honor and principle who was slain.

The Bang-Jensen tragedy has been examined at some length because, better than many pages of analysis it shows the attitudes which are paralyzing America. It may be instructive to pair the events around Bang-Jensen with another slightly similar happening in an unpolitical area, the incident of Marie Torre. As you probably remember, since the newspapers on this occasion gave the story heavy coverage, Marie Torre was a radio and TV gossip columnist who refused to reveal her sources of information on some rumors she had printed about a movie star. When she "bravely" served ten days in jail rather than betray her informants, she was praised by the press for her "courage" and her "rugged adherence to principle."

The American people have not lost their attachment to principle; they have merely become fatuous. They are so paralyzed by the Soviet strategy of threat and terror that Bang-Jensen's protection of men and women from torture and death had to pass unnoticed. But Marie

Torre, who was simply looking out for a fellow gossiper who might have landed in a libel suit, was acclaimed a heroine.

"The greatest tyranny has the smallest beginnings," wrote the London *Times* more than a century ago. "From precedents overlooked, from remonstrations despised, from grievances treated with ridicule, from powerless men oppressed with impunity, and overbearing men tolerated with complacence, springs the tyrannical usage which wise and good men may hereafter perceive and lament and resist in vain."

CHAPTER VIII

THREAT AND TERROR,
BUT WHAT LIES BEHIND THEM?

When I was sixteen years old I went to a citizens' military training camp and there, like many other boys, got my first taste of military life. During that time I happened to see a boxing match put on by two recruits. I never forgot it.

One of the contestants was big, about six feet two, with broad shoulders, long arms, and big muscles. He was a braggart and most of the fellows were afraid of him. The other was small, but superbly conditioned. In uniform he didn't look like much, but as he stepped into the ring you could see that he was in perfect training and that he approached the match with confidence, even though he was outweighed by some sixty pounds, and his reach was possibly five inches shorter than that of his adversary.

The big fellow advanced arrogantly on his little opponent. Suddenly there was a flurry of fists and the little man was pummelling him from every direction. The big fellow didn't land a single solid punch, and it was obvious when the first round ended that he was neither in good condition nor a well-trained boxer. In the first few seconds of the second round his smaller opponent, weaving, bobbing, and banging away with lefts and rights knocked him silly. The referee stopped the fight. It was all over.

Today, in the international field we have a situation much like that boxing match. We have a big, well-propagandized Soviet Union and the smaller, quieter but superbly trained and skilled United States. Americans, and people throughout the world have been told repeatedly by Soviet propaganda of the immense Soviet strength, their rising production, their rockets, and their plans to "bury us" with their overwhelming economic and military power. But an intelligent person who would seriously give time and study to examining the on-the-spot investigations and actual reports of American and foreign experts in economic and military areas would discover material facts which would astonish him. He would see that the average American has been completely misled as to the true nature of the contrast between American and Soviet power. Soviet propaganda about the threat of Russian military and economic achievements is too easily believed. Even without examining the evidence, a little common sense will note right in the beginning that propaganda is always larger than fact. Whatever strength the Russians actually possess is sure to be blown up by their skillful experts to a hundred times true size. That is their job. A good measure of their capacity to inflate belief over actuality is the "economic warfare" campaign. Remember in the chapter on world trade, how drastically the comparative force of the so-called economic threat shrank before the verified figures?

General George Patton, early in World War II, was asked why he was not discouraged at the vaunted strength and skill of the German armies. He replied, "I have studied the German for forty years. I have read the memoirs of his great men. I have studied every detail of his military campaigns. I have attended some of his staff courses. I know exactly how he will react under any given set of circumstances. He does not know what I will do. For this reason, when the time comes, I shall beat the hell out of him." And that is exactly what Patton did.

There are people in the United States who have made just as thorough studies of Soviet Communism and Soviet strategy and tactics and Soviet economics and Soviet military power for the past twenty years. They know Soviet strength and they know Soviet weaknesses. From these hard-eyed experts on Soviet promise and actual Soviet performance, and not from Soviet propaganda bureaus, comes the truth. As was tellingly stated in a recent report to Congress on Soviet tactics: "The greatest asset the Communists have at the present time is not the hydrogen bomb, not Soviet satellites, but world ignorance of their tactics, strategy and objectives."[1] The world is particularly ignorant of the true state of Soviet economic and military affairs, and it has been a vital part of Soviet strategy to keep the ignorance at as high a level as possible.

Consider first the basic economic fabric of life in the Soviet Union. Professor G. Warren Nutter, associate professor of economics at the University of Virginia, visited Russia in 1956.[2] He traveled throughout the country and saw many industrial plants and collective farms. He visited many Soviet executives. His over-all conclusions about Soviet industrial capacity were that "Russia's economy . . . is half a century behind the West." As for Russian airplanes, cars, radios, and modern weapons, he calls these "anachronisms in a country that is, by and large, still backward." He saw a plant one hundred and twenty years old, manufacturing curtains with European machines dating from 1886, and paying wages of 600 to 1000 rubles a month. Figuring the value of the ruble at the rate of twenty-four to a dollar, that means incomes were between $25 and $50 a month. In a machine-tool plant designed and built by American engineers in 1934, the equipment was all foreign. Its tools were of "good quality" but "cruder than comparable Western models." But he also noted that the "technology of the plant still seemed to be geared to its original design, now over twenty years old . . . safety equipment was totally absent; and almost no automatic hand tools were in use."

Nutter estimated that the technology in Soviet light

industry was between fifteen and seventy years behind the United States. Instead of using wheelbarrows they are using sledges and two-man litters. The farmers use scythes instead of mowers, and brooms are still made of bundles of twigs. Whenever he saw an item which appeared new, it was usually a copy of a foreign model, like the automobile Zis, which is a copy of a 1939 Packard; or the Zim, which is a copy of the 1939 Buick; or the Zil, which was introduced in 1957 and is patterned after the Cadillacs of about 1940. Other automobiles copy early Plymouths and Ramblers. Electric shavers, vacuum cleaners, calculating machines, and motor busses were all copied directly from American, Swedish, German, and Austrian models.

Speaking of Soviet housing, Professor Nutter said, "Picture the slums of any major American city and magnify them to occupy nine tenths of the city. That is the nature of Soviet housing." Of bricklaying he reported that their methods had not changed in fifty years. In excavating for buildings, work forces were using shovels instead of bulldozers.

Here are the estimates made by Nutter as an expert on economics of the comparative levels of United States and Soviet production: In steel, Russia is twenty-nine years behind the United States; in electric power, sixteen years behind; in coal, forty-seven years behind the United States; oil, thirty-four years behind; natural gas, fifty-two years behind; fertilizer, sixteen years behind; and paper production, fifty-four years behind our own achievement. All figures are based on official Soviet and United States reports of production.

In the production of cement, Russia is thirty-two years behind; rails, fifty-four years behind; rail passenger cars, fifty-three years behind; and freight cars, sixty-nine years behind. In butter production they are thirty-five years behind; and in shoes, forty-four years behind. In canned food they are forty-five years behind; and wool fabrics, sixty-nine years behind the United States.

"Domestic airplanes, except for the one famous jet, are all two engined, non-pressurized models fashioned after the DC–3."

Professor Nutter, seeing many large projects in various stages of completion, concluded that many big, new Soviet works are done chiefly for show. "One quickly gets the feeling that the Russians have an obsession about making a good impression. Hence great attention has been paid to creating a pleasant façade covering and obscuring, in a literal sense, the unpleasant sights." This façade is what most Americans see when they go to the Soviet Union and report back on the "tremendous progress." They see the showplaces. Indeed that is what the leaders in the Soviet Union want their own people to see. Looking at the great Moscow subway station, the new buildings, and the parks, they are to be less conscious of the nine tenths of the Soviet cities that are slums, and the factories still working as they did fifty or a hundred years ago. Morale and propaganda are the purposes of this type of production.

The average Russian city dweller has six times less income than the average American although everything he buys is between six and one hundred times more expensive than a corresponding item bought by his American counterpart. According to Lawrence Sullivan, Coordinator of Information for the House of Representatives, eggs in Moscow sell for $6.60 a dozen, a woolen suit costs $2,940.00, a pair of shoes costs $130.20.

In 1958 the estimated food production per capita in the Soviet Union according to the Department of Agriculture's World Food Survey, was eight per cent *lower* than their prewar average. Before the revolution, Russia *exported* large amounts of wheat. By 1956 it was *importing* fifteen million bushels a year. To the Soviet Party Congress in January, 1959, Khrushchev complained that Soviet collectivized agriculture was using more than seven times as much labor to produce grain as the United States, over five times more labor to grow potatoes, over six times as much to grow beets, over fourteen times as much to raise cattle, over sixteen times as much to raise pigs. According to the Population Reference Bureau, 52 per cent of the Soviet population work on farms. In the United States only about twelve million people work on farms, less than 10 per cent of our population. In farming, the Soviet Union is about where the United States was soon after the Civil War.

The Assembly of Captive European Nations in a documented report, *Soviet Empire: 1917-1958,* points out that thirty-one million citizens earn between $600 and $900

115

a year, while one hundred sixty million Soviet citizens earn less than $600 a year. Only about three hundred thousand have an income larger than $6,000 a year. In addition to this very low and poor living standard there are an estimated six million to twenty-eight million Soviet workers in slave labor camps, who earn between nothing and $25 a month.

Workers in the captive states are no better off. According to a study made by the Department of International Affairs—AFL–CIO, the living standards are today lower than they were in 1938. In Albania, for instance, it takes a worker over an hour to earn enough money to buy a pound of flour. It took him only twenty minutes in 1938. In Poland it takes twenty minutes to earn a pound of bread compared to ten minutes in 1938, and compared to five minutes today in the United States. In Red Hungary it takes more than two hundred hours to earn money for a new suit compared with a little more than thirty hours in the United States. Claims made for the rise of living standards in the Soviet Union and the captive nations are almost entirely mythical. *Fortune* magazine in March 1959 made an estimate of future production increase in the United States during the 1960s. Its figures showed that *just the increase* of American production in the 1960s will be almost as much as the entire present national production of the Soviet Union and West Germany combined. This expected increase will come to no less than $250,000,000,000, a 50 per cent increase in ten years, which will be the largest percentage production in any decade of our history. It was quite accurate when Milovan Djilas, the Yugoslav ex-Communist leader who smuggled out of prison his devastating book, the *New Class*, described the Communist system, which he had helped institute and under which he had lived, as the most wasteful economy in the history of human society.

It seems impossible that any reasonable critic could compare the Soviet system favorably with our own. Yet when Khrushchev announced his new seven-year plan with its tremendous production goals, there were commentators in the United States whose critical sense had apparently been entirely suspended by the Soviet propaganda offensive. Edward R. Murrow warned solemnly that the Soviets were out to conquer the world by economic production.[3] He did not mention—if he even knew —that the new seven-year plan was put into effect because the then operating five-year plan, which was not even finished, had failed so drastically to meet its quotas that it had to be discarded, as the Soviet Union's own statistics proved.

Michael Padev, the same foreign editor who helped interview Bang-Jensen, went to Russia last year with Vice-President Nixon's party. He speaks fluent Russian and was therefore able to see and hear more at first hand than correspondents who had to be guided by Communist officials. He saw factories, visited homes, and spoke to taxi drivers, professors, and workmen. His conclusion, as a trained observer and reporter after this relatively close contact with the actual Russian environment was

117

that "in economic development Russia is today decades behind Western Europe, let alone the United States. . . . I visited one of the largest Soviet dams and electric power stations as well as one of the most modern Soviet machine tool factories near the Siberian city of Novosibersk. I also visited the docks on the Russian Baltic port of Leningrad. I saw some factories and plants in Moscow and Sverdlovsk—the pride of post-war Soviet planners. . . . I found conditions everywhere truly primitive. I would say without exaggeration that in methods of work, of workmanship, in technical know-how, industrial efficiency and labor productivity, today's Russia is years behind Eastern Europe before World War II [Padev was a native of Bulgaria]. And pre-war Eastern Europe was considered a comparatively underdeveloped part of Europe. . . .

"The factories themselves are also old-fashioned, backward, and primitive to an almost unbelievable extent. Workers, dressed in tattered old clothes, . . . walk about and work in dirty, dusty, and dark alleys, with primitive tools and almost no comfort. Their manufactured products can be described in one word, 'shoddy,' and that goes for everything from passenger cars and tractors to ball-pens and tooth brushes. . . .

"Russia now is perhaps the richest state in the world in terms of natural resources. Under such excellent conditions the Communists have built one of the worst economic systems in the world."

Padev compared notes with engineers, workers and

118

professors on salaries and living expenses in Russia: "The average good salary of a qualified worker is about 800 rubles a month. A senior engineer would get over 2,000 rubles. An Intourist guide, which is considered an excellent job, makes 1,000 rubles a month.

"A bad pair of men's shoes costs 350 rubles.

"A very poor quality of men's shirt: more than 300 rubles.

"An average meal for two in a good restaurant: 80 rubles.

"A clumsily built old fashioned radio: 1,500 rubles. That's more than a month's salary for most workers."[4]

People in the United States are being fooled again and again both by Soviet propaganda and by unwitting American and European writers who are ignorant of true facts. The danger, of course, is that we will soon believe the Soviet Union is so strong that we will be afraid to oppose any demand made by Khrushchev. This is precisely the aim of Soviety strategy.

But, you might say, Russian economic strength is not the real threat. The real threat is the rockets and H-Bombs. What about the Russian armies in Europe and Asia? Wars are not won with economics, they are won with weapons.

This is true. But why should Soviet claims for missiles and rockets be more accurate in relation to actual facts, than the claims for trade expansion reviewed in Chapter V, or the economic claims examined above? The Soviet Union has much more to gain by inflating the world's image of its military prowess than it can gain from exaggerated world images in regard to trade and economy. We can be sure that their efforts to inflate their military image are double and treble the propaganda efforts they are making in other directions.

Reports by military experts betray a gap of gigantic proportions between the world's idea of Russian military might and the logical deductions which fit known facts. Wing Commander Asher Lee, Royal Air Force expert and author of *Soviet Air and Rocket Forces,* recently made a flat statement that the Soviet Union cannot hit the United States with any rocket it now has, or will have in the near future.[5] Its bombers, because of their short range, are not capable of attacking the United States directly. The United States has a much larger fleet of experienced jet bombers to attack the Soviet Union. Furthermore, Commander Lee does not believe that Russians, with their present capabilities, can develop any effective defense against the Strategic Air Command of the United States with its present resources.

In the field of air transport, says Commander Lee, the Tupelov 114 is the biggest transport in the world today, but it is not the best. The Boeing 707 is faster and carries more weight for its size. The design of the Tupelov is a make-over of the Soviet Bear, which is nothing more than a copy of the American B-29, whose design the Soviets secured during World War II, when two of these planes had to land in Siberia after attacking Japan. According to Commander Lee, the Tupelov 114 is already obsolescent. It is primarily a demonstration aircraft made to impress foreigners. It will never go into regular passenger service.

Thus, the British expert, Commander Lee.

It is perfectly possible, of course, that Commander Lee may be wrong. Military experts have been mistaken in the past, and some will be mistaken again. But is it more sensible to give weight to Commander Lee, whose every interest lies in evaluating the facts and relaying them accurately, or to prefer to believe the claims carefully disseminated by the Russians, whose favorite boast is that they are the world's best propagandists and who are convinced that their own survival depends on their being thought all-powerful?

Commander Lee is strongly supported by his American counterparts. Testifying before Congress in March 1959, Admiral Arleigh Burke stated that in any all-out war "we can destroy Russia many times over with the weapons we now have in existence. There is no way that she can stop that. We could break her back."

General Maxwell D. Taylor testified that the United States "already has too much atomic retaliatory power. We have thousands of vehicles which could rain nuclear destruction of the Soviets whereas the job could be done with hundreds."

Air Force General Nathan F. Twining stated that any Soviet assault would have to come from manned aircraft. Russia's airpower is "not half as big as ours and not nearly so effective." The United States can deliver nuclear bombs from airplanes with accuracy measured in feet, compared to the miles expected from long-range missiles. And American Thor missiles, already operational in 1959, could hit the Soviet Union with atomic warheads from bases in Britain.

In July 1959 a paper drafted privately by a group of top military officers in Washington was circulated to various leading officials of the government.[6] It stated that some State Department officials were advising Secretary of State Christian Herter to yield to the Soviet Union at the Geneva conference because United States military power was declining compared to that of Russia. The officers declared vigorously in their circular that the allegation was entirely untrue. True or untrue, it is certainly what the Russians would like to have any American Secretary of State believe, particularly at a time when he is about to face them for a prolonged and much publicized set of discussions.

One excellent way to appraise the Soviet military situation realistically is to suppose that the tables are turned, and it is we who are in the Soviet position. We would face the following menaces: There would be more than two thousand modern Soviet fighters, all better than ours, stationed at two hundred and fifty bases in Mexico and the Caribbean. Overwhelming Russian naval power would be always within a few hundred miles of our coasts. Half of the population of the United States would be needed to work on farms just to feed the people. It is not ourselves, however, but the Soviet Union which is in this position. If a war should start, the Soviet Union would be virtually helpless, with captive peoples in Hungary, Poland, East Germany, Czechoslovakia, Romania, Bulgaria, Estonia, Latvia, Lithuania, and Albania all ready to revolt the minute the terror of internal security control slackened because of necessary withdrawal of Russian forces for the front.

The revolt in Hungary and the near revolt in Poland prove that the peoples of captive nations will rise to throw off the Communist yoke whenever there is a possibility of success. Khrushchev's bitterest complaint to Vice-President Nixon was that "Captive Nations Week" was celebrated in the United States at the same time that the Vice-President took off on his trip to Moscow. Khrushchev knows that he is holding in check by sheer force the explosive power of enraged populations, ready to strike from behind at the first opportunity. He knows, too, that the Soviet Union cannot be defended from the Strategic Air Command's supersonic bomber fleet. His second complaint to Nixon concerned the two hundred and fifty airbases which ring the Soviet Union. The force radiating from these bases is massive and unstoppable. Soviet efforts in diplomacy and propaganda concentrate intensively on these two facts, which in actuality hold the Soviet Union in a tight military trap—the fury of the captive nations, and the iron ring of American bases. Every move of the Soviet Union has as its background the effort to portray the captive nations as "independent." They are to be regarded by the world as autonomous countries with whose "internal affairs" the imperialistic United States must not meddle. Always implicit is the threat that interference may require the Soviet Union to go to the "defense" of these countries and thus trigger World War III. The American bases are portrayed as a vicious menace to world peace, because they make the "great peaceful" Soviet Union feel threatened, force her to arm, and may force her into atomic war by some nebulous process supposed to be connected with self-defense. The bases themselves—in some way always left equally nebulous in these explanations—are supposed to be always about to cause the unleashing of the unspeakable horror of the Third World War. The fact is, however, that Khrushchev wants this cataclysmic war even less than we, for he is far more vulnerable. But if he can terrify the world into supposing he is apt to plunge into war at any moment as a result of these circumstances, he is immediately in the position of being able to put upon us great pressure from our allies and our citizens. If he can pressure us into giving up our bases and also into abandoning the captive nations, he will have taken from both ourselves and the free world the two weapons most necessary to survival. Without striking a blow in actuality, he will have made a gigantic step forward toward Communist world domination, which, if it comes, will be as irreversible in the world as it has been in the separate nations which it has taken over. But as long as the United States openly supports the eventual liberation of the captive states, and as long as American airpower can "break the back" of Russian military might, both we and the free world have nothing to fear from the Soviet Union. These are the facts. If we know the truth about our strength and Soviet weakness, *and act upon it,* there is no force on earth which can prevail against us.

Much is made of the giant strides the Soviet Union is said to have taken in the conquest of space and in missile development. In considering Soviet claims, however, two facts should always be kept in mind. The first is that the problem is not one of absolute power on the Soviet side or upon our own, but of relative power. As long as we are able to destroy the Soviet Union, if the Soviet Union should attempt to destroy us, peace has the maximum chance of being kept. But if we let down our guard and allow the Soviets to equal or surpass us in military power, war and eventual world surrender to Communism become inevitable. The more one-sided the balance becomes, the greater is the danger of war; for the stronger the antagonist is, the less apt he is to be deterred by fear of retaliation.

The second fact to remember is that the Russians, who are masters of propaganda, are constantly eager to have us believe that the balance is tipping decisively to their side. They believe they can, in this way, sap our will to resist. Tremendous fanfare surrounds such feats as the flights of the luniks and the recent firing of the Soviet long-range missile into the Pacific. Contemplating these claims, the Western World is supposed to tremble. The horror of atomic war, which throughout the West is being widely dramatized by television and movies and fiction, is supposed to press fear and horror ever deeper into Western consciousness until the will to resist simply melts away. We are to arrive at a frame of mind in which we will be so horrified by terror of atomic war that we will abandon our atomic weapons regardless of circumstances, regardless of whether or not any proposed system of inspection can be circumvented by the Russians. This attitude would, of course, be suicide. Only military superiority backed by firm will can: (1) prevent war and (2) save the West from Communist domination. Those are facts which should be obvious to even the most rudimentary perception. No one wants atomic weapons, just as no one wants atomic war. But the surest way to bring about atomic war is by hasty and reckless abandonment of the existing balance between ourselves and the Soviet Union. It is because Russia wants to terrify the rest of the world into believing that the balance is indeed swinging fatally to her side, and the danger of the Third World War is steadily growing, that she attempts to outstrip us in the atomic race and so widely publicizes her luniks and her missiles.

In this regard, the truth is that we always have very little evidence about such matters as the lunik flights beyond the information put out by the official Soviet agencies, whose desire is to make us think as highly as possible of Russian accomplishment. Our information about missiles, such as the recent shot into the Pacific, for example, is even more meager. We can be certain, however, that the Soviet Union is straining every propaganda agency at its command to paralyze us with fear.

While we know so little about the actual facts of the Soviet arsenal, however, we know quite clearly the truth about our own defense. The truth is that we do at present possess the power to destroy the Soviet Union if it attacks us. As long as we possess this power, we shall not be attacked. If for even a moment we cease to possess it, we will at once be in grave peril. It seems incredible that so simple and obvious an equation should be in danger of slipping from the view of the American public. There are subtle and powerful currents at work upon all Western opinion to obscure perception of the truth upon which both peace and Western survival depend.

Do we indeed possess the capacity to destroy the Soviet Union if we are attacked? Does the balance actually exist? The factual clarity of the American deterrent power is in sharp contrast to the foggy exaggeration which surrounds typical Soviet missile rattling.

No one should be in a better position to know American missile capacity than Dr. Wernher von Braun. In a recent address, he said, "The Jupiter program is just about finished so far as the development phase is concerned. We gave the country an IRBM capability in the relatively short time of three years. . . . Now that missile system is being deployed in Italy . . . . backed up by other missile systems of our NATO forces on the Continent . . .

127

Jupiter can deliver its awesome destructive power against any target within its range of more than 1,500 nautical miles.

"Also deployed with the U.S. Army forces in Europe is another of our missile systems, the Redstone. . . . While it has a lesser range than its big brother, the Jupiter, the Redstone can transport a very heavy warhead with great reliability and uncanny accuracy."[7]

What other missiles do we have? The 1,500-mile Polaris missile which can be shot from atomic submarines into any part of the Soviet Union has been perfected. It could also be shot from land bases and moved into place by railroad cars. Each Polaris could blow up an entire Soviet city. We will have 32 of them operational by the end of 1960.

We have the 9,000-mile Atlas and the Titan, 130 of the first under production and 140 of the second, which can be shot into the Soviet Union from Vandenberg Air Force Base in California.

The Thor missile is already operational and is based in England. Others are being based in Turkey. It is a medium range missile, already perfected. Plans in 1960 called for 120 of these in Western Europe.

If plans are fully carried out, and past experience proves this virtually certain, there will be 518 Polaris, Thor, Atlas, Titan, Redstone, and Jupiter missiles all set to hit the Soviet Union, if necessary, by 1962. Added to this the United States has over 1,500 supersonic bombers that can rain nuclear destruction on Russia with pinpoint accuracy from 250 bases all over the world. There is no evidence that the Soviet Union has anti-aircraft defenses capable of stopping them.

General Nathan Twining, Chairman of the Joint Chiefs of Staff, testified before Congress last February 9: "On the basis of all the information available to me, and in view of the mission and location of our retaliatory weapons systems, I just do not believe that any nation possesses the ability today or in the foreseeable future to attack us or destroy us without receiving unacceptable damage in return."[8]

Make the comparison yourself. Is there a balance of power between Russia and the Western World? We know that the Soviet Union may have shot a missile 7,760 miles into the Pacific. We know that they claim to have intercontinental missiles that can bring severe damage to the United States. That is all we know about the true extent of their missile strength.

But we know that in actual and verifiable fact the United States has missiles in operation with the Navy, Air Force, and Army in Europe and in the United States. We know we have 1,500 planes loaded with nuclear weapons which can destroy the entire Soviet Union. These are not claims; they are facts testified to under oath before Congress by our military leaders.

It is often said that it is dangerous to underestimate your enemy. That danger is obvious. Less obvious, however, is the danger which comes from overestimating the enemy, particularly when it is the enemy's obvious wish that you shall suffer the highest possible fear of his threats. America is experiencing a draining away of her will and is being tempted to abandon the balance of power. The brutal fact remains that it is the existence of the balance of power which keeps the peace, and until some genuinely workable system of disarmament is devised, the one-sided abandon of the balance of power is the surest possible way to plunge the world into extinction in World War III.

There were significant aspects of the recent U2 flights over Soviet territory which were not emphasized in most headlines. One is the fact that flights continued over Soviet bases for four years before a plane was brought down, although the Russians were by their own admission aware of their passage. Obviously those U2s could not be reached by any rockets the Soviets had, or they would have scored a hit long before this. Another point is that the Soviet leaders were perfectly aware that their installations were being photographed but made no protest until publicizing the spectacular shooting down of the last U2 was so much to their advantage in the cold war that they broke the silence. Russia was very anxious not to let the West know that such overflights were militarily possible, for the propaganda about her invincible rockets was too important to disturb. To Russia, propaganda is central. It was only when the propaganda value of breaking secrecy became greater than the propaganda value of continuing to be silent, that Russia made its protests. The U2 episode is a startling illustration of the intensity with which the Soviet Union wages propaganda and pursues the cold war. It is an attitude almost incredible to the West, whose free press bluntly reports events as they happen. If the West could just understand the nature of Russian propaganda and divorce it from the Western handling of "news," the Soviet Union would lose one of its strongest weapons.

The question of whether or not the U2 flights were justified is an extremely difficult one. As a police state, Russia can surround her launching bases for atomic missiles with a secrecy no free nation can duplicate. Russia is constantly boasting of her power to "annihilate" us from these bases. It therefore seems beyond doubt necessary for us to know where the bases are located, and a good case can be made for the contention that if our government did not use every practicable means of securing such knowledge, it would be an almost criminal failure of responsibility toward defense of our own citizens and the free world. A widespread reaction among many Americans to the publicity surrounding the flights of the U2 was an expression of relief that we were really "doing something." "I didn't know," said one man, "that our intelligence was that good." People realize that our intelligence has to be good. Our survival depends on it.

On the other hand, the official handling of the last U2 flight was inept almost beyond belief, and there was surely never a keener contrast between Soviet mastery of propaganda and our own clumsiness. There was first a conventional assertion that the U2 was engaged in weather reconnaissance, then a retraction, and finally an admission of the U2's true nature. There is the further point that if Russia began similar flights over the United States, we would make every effort in our power to end them, because obviously such a flight might carry nuclear bombs. Russia's reaction is much the same as our own would be. Therefore, it is difficult to seem to blame her.

Where the blame actually lies is with the secrecy, the truculence, and the proclamation of destructive goals which the Soviet Union continually imposes upon the world. Her leaders are trying to terrorize their way into the same absolute power over the entire globe as they have within their own tragic country. Every deterrent which the West possesses must be used, whether it is intelligence or build-up of military defense. At the same time, care must be taken not to trigger the very conflict we are trying to avoid. But the surest possible way to set that conflict off and turn the cold war into a hot one is to allow Russia to make us believe it is so strong that only a series of abject submissions can save us from annihilation.

Since the rise of Communist China, a great deal has been heard about the peril which threatens us from this new quarter. Suppose one could convince a would-be appeaser of Communism of the truth about Soviet military capacity, and prove that we could overwhelm the Russians with ease. He would then instantly add that, with China now on the Russian side, all these appraisals must be erased because the danger has been vastly increased.

Russia is always quick to demonstrate solidarity with Communist China. Repressing their obvious differences and frequent mutual mistrust, the Soviet Union wants to present to the world not only a picture of unity, but of China as a formidable ally, an overwhelming addition to the strength of the Russian camp. Therefore, in replying to the Russian threat one must also reply to the Chinese threat. What are the facts about China?

Communist China has an enormous population, but population is a weakness rather than a strength among the swarming Asian nations. China's estimated six hundred million people, according to Dr. Sripati Chandrasekhar, Director of the Indian Institute of Population Studies in Madras, last year reproduced themselves at the rate of twenty-four million. That is not just twenty-four million potential soldiers. It is twenty-four million mouths to feed, bodies to house, people to find jobs for. Birth control has been tried and has failed. China is too primitive and too poor to make large scale use of birth control.

The Chinese Communist government has acknowledged that its claims for increased production in agriculture and industry have been fraudulent. On August 26 last year the Party Central Committee admitted that the boasts of record-breaking production from farms and factories had been based on false statistics. As a result they set their goals for 1959 at figures which were sometimes less than half of what had been claimed as actual production for the previous year. The wheat quota for 1959 was cut from five hundred and twenty-five million to two hundred and seventy-five million tons. Steel production was cut from eighteen million to twelve million tons. The committee admitted that the highly touted "backyard furnace" program which was supposed to increase Chinese steel production had been a complete failure and was being abandoned. The cotton production goal was cut from four and a half-million tons to two and a half-million.

Investment of capital construction has been reduced, coal-mine quotas have been cut, and the estimate of total industrial production was reduced from 165,000,000,000 yuan to 147,000,000,000 yuan or about $58,000,000,000 at Red China's own rate of exchange. American industrial production is over $450,000,000,000 and we have one hundred and seventy-five million people instead of six hundred million.

One of the most accurate and complete recent investigations of Communist China by an outsider was made last year by Louis Wiznitzer, American correspondent for "Diario de Noticias" of Rio de Janeiro. Wiznitzer, who spent two months in Red China, presents a picture of Chinese Communism which indicates an even greater gap between fact and propaganda than Professor Nutter's findings for the Soviet Union. Wiznitzer reports that Chinese industrial power is "practically nonexistent."[9]

China has plenty of men for its armies, but has no modern military capability and cannot have because there is no industrial base. As was true at the time of Korea, all effective equipment must come from the Soviet Union.

The plants that Russia has built directly for the Red Chinese to operate are not successful. For example, Wiznitzer saw an oil refinery which had six cracking towers. Five were deserted, the sixth was working, but at only a fraction of capacity. He was told the plant was in operation, but that nothing was being produced. Wiznitzer who had been prepared to be impressed by the great advances he had heard had been made by the Communists in China, instead came away with the conviction that 95 per cent of Red China is as primitive as any nation on earth and that the claims for great advances in agriculture and industry were completely unfounded. There is "no transportation at all, as we know it," no trucks or tractors—just men's backs. Nearly all the machinery the Chinese have comes from Russia, and most of it is not operating. There are no modern assembly lines. What production there was, resulted from handwork. The Chinese, according to Wiznitzer, are actually producing almost nothing. Instead of taking off 25 per cent or 50 per cent from claimed Chinese production figures, he says, we in many cases should take off 99 per cent. Swedish experts who have been helping to build a steel plant in Shanghai say that the claimed production of the Chinese for this plant, one million tons, is actually only two hundred thousand, and that even if the plant were operating at full capacity it could produce only three hundred and fifty thousand tons.

Is this the powerful new Communist force which is supposed to be raising the Soviet threat to the West to dazzling new magnitude? Clearly, for the present, the claim is ridiculous. China is a paper dragon. Yet there are many people who believe in China's might and want to add appeasing Mao to our other appeasements. They urge admission of Communist China to the United Nations. They beg for avoidance of offense to Chinese leaders, just as offense is avoided in regard to Khrushchev. And yet there are good reasons now to believe that if we had had the resolution, on any of several occasions in the past, to back the Nationalist Chinese or the South Koreans in diversionary offensives against the Communist Chinese, we could have achieved—perhaps not complete liberation—but at least some steps toward it. We could have helped create the sort of stubborn stalemate plus infiltration with which the Russians themselves have been so successful in disrupting portions of Asia. Nor would any such incident have flared into global war, for the same reason that the several similar situations in Asia do not grow into direct war between the West and the Soviet Union. No one wants global war. No one will risk it. The Russians make use of this fact, nibble at our perimeters with their limited offensives, and by the threat of direct war keep us from effective counteraction. But this procedure can work both ways.

In the nuclear age, threats and psychological offensive

can play a role which in the past could be enforced only by guns. The classic aim of all strategy is to take from the enemy what you want and make him unable to take what he wants. If fear of the enemy, of his weapons, of what he might do to explode nuclear war, causes us to give him whatever he wants and makes us unable to secure anything we want, our cause is already being lost as surely as if we were suffering repeated defeats in battle. Dr. Robert Strausz-Hupé,[10] Director of the Foreign Policy Research Institute, describes the Communist technique accurately when he says that "by projecting an exaggerated image of their strength" the Communists "inhibit the Western response to their carefully calibrated challenges. . . . It is as dangerous to overestimate Communist power as to underestimate it. The penalty for overestimation is invariably relinquishment of the initiative to the enemy."

Suppose, however, against all the evidence, that the experts are wrong—that the Soviet Union did surpass and continued to surpass the United States in the total sum of military power, as the would-be appeasers claim. If this were indeed the fact, what would be the intelligent course for us to adopt? Would it be to squander our treasure, surrender our liberties and those of our friends, and teach the world to despise us for our weakness? Or would it be to strengthen our military might, defend our friends, and make our courage and integrity feared by our enemy and respected by those whose inclination is to stand at our side?

Too many people in the United States have surrendered weakly to the Soviet psychological offensive. Only twice in recent years have we actually called a Soviet bluff—once in Quemoy and once in Lebanon. On both occasions the enemy backed down. He will back down every time—in Berlin, the Middle East, the Far East, anywhere. We have only to knock the chip off his shoulder, and he is suddenly quiet. He knows who has the stronger force: economic, political, ethical, military, and every other. It is we who are not sure. With great cunning he has exploited our growing weakness of character to create in us this dangerous uncertainty. It is time we saw ourselves as the enemy sees us, formidable and in fact unbeatable.

CHAPTER IX

THE UNITED NATIONS:
INSTRUMENT FOR PEACE
OR FORUM FOR WAR?

"No man is an island." These words come from the pen of the Elizabethan poet John Donne. They have been put into pleasantly warm, up-to-date ballads, popular in organizations which stress nation-to-nation friendship. They express the emotional fervor, the call to international togetherness which is the spirit behind the intense and uncritical enthusiasm of some of the world's nicest people for the United Nations. All men are brothers according to this ideal—brothers united in a great world organization which is the one true hope for peace and understanding in today's world.

This idea is, of course, not new. It has been the hope of the utopian thinkers from the time of Plato through Sir Thomas More to Woodrow Wilson. It is an ideal, however, which has never become a reality. Yet millions of people all over the world hope for it, believe in it, and work for it. And because they have hoped so hard, and believed so deeply, many of them have become convinced that the ideal has at last become a fact, and that in the United Nations the world has truly achieved a working and sincere international community.

It is this wishful illusion about the United Nations that has today grown into a powerful emotional and intellectual force. Millions of Americans, influenced by the floods of partisan writings by apologists for the United Nations and by groups supporting the ideal of international unity, also believe that in the United Nations rests the greatest hope for world peace. The wish is, of course, the father to the thought. And it is not unnatural that people of good faith should want so badly to believe that the United Nations is the final solution to the conflicts which rend the world, that they cling to their belief in spite of the accumulating evidence that, far from being a force for world peace, the United Nations is, in fact, a forum for war.

Thus there is today a wide gap between what is true and what is believed to be true. Many suppose that the United Nations is really "united," just as many also suppose that the term "mutual security" is an accurate label, although, as we have seen, the program is neither "mutual" nor "secure." Similarly, the new Soviet slogan "peace and friendship," developed to apply to a policy which is neither peaceful nor friendly, and the famous Soviet "dove of peace" is in truth about as far from the true nature of the Soviet Union as any symbol could possibly be. We have entered a period in which so many facts are masquerading under labels proclaiming them to be the exact opposite of what they really are that we are currently not far from the situation satirized by George Orwell in his brilliant novel *1984*, where the secret police are called the Ministry of Love, and the offices of propaganda are labelled the Ministry of Truth.

The theory of the "United Nations" belongs to the same general category as the one Orwell satirizes. In the United Nations all the peoples of the earth are said to be marching together towards a better, brighter future. Hand in hand, all are joining in the common effort.

But effort towards what?

And hand and hand with whom?

With Khrushchev?

Certainly there are many who at present believe that with Khrushchev some sort of union, or at least "friendly competition," is indeed possible. Is not Khrushchev a far better man than Stalin? Has he not lessened tensions? Does he not constantly talk about peace and friendship? Isn't it perfectly possible that he can really be persuaded to lead his people into the new era of international togetherness and thus relieve the fears of the world?

Let us suppose, for the sake of illustration, that it were the Hitler of Nazi Germany who was being discussed instead of Khrushchev in this context. Would anyone today for even a moment seriously suppose that Hitler and his bloodstained regime would actually work for peace through an organization of international brotherhood like the United Nations? Most of those who now sincerely believe that the United Nations must be the cornerstone of American foreign policy are the very same people who recoiled in horror at the crimes of Hitler: the concentration camps, the torture and murder of the millions of Jews, the genocide he practiced with brutal efficiency, the aggression and slavery to which he subjected Germany's neighbors. Would they, could they, in the light of what is known today about the German dictator's psychology, believe that such a man as Hitler could ever be counted on to join in a United Nations effort toward common goals of peace and friendship? Would they not instead be certain that Hitler would use his membership in the United Nations to further his own plans of conquest, to advance his dream of world power, and to impose the Nazi regime upon as much of the world as he could? But Khrushchev is different from Hitler, people will say.

Is he?

When Khrushchev was visiting the United States in the fall of 1959, and while he was being pictured smiling and joking, holding up a big yellow ear of corn—while this scene was being played out in Iowa, quite a different set of events was taking place in Washington. The House of Representatives was holding hearings. There were only brief accounts in the newspapers, because their pages were too tightly filled with the extensive coverage of the Soviet Premier's visit. The reports of the hearings were given little space and went largely unnoticed.

But what did they contain?

Listen.

Mykold Lebed, leader of the Ukrainian liberation movement against the Hitler occupation from 1941 to 1943, is speaking of the methods used by the Soviet government after the war against those Ukrainians in whom the underground resistance to Hitler had roused a taste for independence:

"These methods were applied not only to prisoners in interrogation rooms and cells, but also in public places, forcing the people to get together to witness these atrocities." [Please remember this is 1944. This is not a nation in the surge of revolutionary fever as in 1917. This is a nation to whom such methods have become part of its permanent way of life.]

"They poisoned medical capsules or medicines which were supposed to be used to cure a patient. In that way, instead of curing him they inflicted certain other diseases which became very widely spread. . . . Also, water for public use was poisoned, cigarettes and chocolate were tampered with in this manner. After consuming them people became sick. . . .

"These methods were applied in order to terrorize the population of Ukraine and depress its will to resist the regime."

Mr. Lebed was asked, "Who was directing the perpetration of these barbarities in the Ukraine?"

"Khrushchev was the man. . . . He was the first secretary of the Central Committee of the Communist Party and the chairman of the council of ministers at that time."

Dr. Lev E. Dobriansky, professor of Soviet economics at Georgetown University read some more of Khrushchev's history into the record: "He was engaged in extensive purges in Ukraine actually to make way for himself to eventually become the first secretary of the Communist Party in Ukraine.

"In these purges he directly engaged in the murder of people like Kossier and others. Countless others met death as a result of Khrushchev's perpetration of these extensive purges. . . . The purges continued during the period of the 30's to wipe out well over 400,000 Ukrainians. . . .

"As first secretary of the Communist Party of the Ukraine he was involved in the heinous massacre of 9,500 Ukrainians in Vinnitsa. . . .

"In 1944-46 Khrushchev was responsible for the liquidation of the Ukrainian Catholic Church, and continued the suppression of the Ukrainian Orthodox Autocephalic Church. He has continued to keep both institutions in extinction. . . .

"In Kingir in 1954, he was responsible, by way of command, for the decimation of five hundred Ukrainian women who protested conditions in the camp." [They were killed by Russian army tanks.]

General Bela Kiraly, former commander of the Hungarian General Staff College, later a prisoner of the Communist Hungarian government, and, during the revolt, commander-in-chief of the National Guard of Hungary, also testified before the committee. He told of the successful revolt of the Hungarian freedom fighters, the ousting of Russian troops from Budapest and the complete victory of the revolution. Then the Russian Ambassador approached the Hungarian government and said, "We have nothing in our minds against the Hungarian people. We sympathize with you. I am ordered by the Soviet government to propose further negotiations with the Hungarian government concerning the details of the withdrawal of the Soviet troops."

The Hungarians accepted. They sent a delegation including Minister of Defense Pal Maleter and Minister of State Erdei. Discussions began. An agreement was reached to withdraw all Soviet troops from Hungary by January fifteenth. Then "The Hungarian delegation entered the Soviet Headquarters with good faith, intending to sign the final text of the Soviet Hungarian agreement. . . . The Hungarian delegation continued their negotiations on the spot. . . .

"About midnight General Serov [of the Soviet secret police] entered the room and, no doubt on the order of Khrushchev, arrested the Hungarian delegation. . . . And from that point they disappeared, we do not know what happened. . . . But I was under treatment of the secret police and can imagine what happened with these persons. . . .

"After that, some of the delegation, more important the Home Defense Minister [Pal Maleter], one of the heads of the delegation, was executed in Hungary in 1958. . . . November 4, 1956, the beginning of the second Soviet aggression and the arrest of General Pal Maleter and the Hungarian diplomatic delegation, is the second 'day of infamy' of modern history."

Soviet troops then invaded the country without warning. The Soviet Ambassador kept telling Premier Imre Nagy that there had been a mistake and no order had been given Soviet troops to march into Hungary. Nagy hesitated and soon found himself facing Russian tanks in front of the capitol. He escaped temporarily to the Yugoslav Embassy. But the Hungarian long-time career Communist Janos Kadar, who still rules Hungary, promised Nagy that he would not be prosecuted for his part in the revolt. Nagy left the Yugoslav Embassy on the strength of this promise. He was then kidnapped by the Soviet soldiers, sent to Rumania, and executed at Khrushchev's orders.

Meanwhile Soviet troops were destroying Budapest. Listen to Joseph Koevago, former mayor of Budapest, describe the scene: "I am an eyewitness who saw with my own eyes that these tanks turned into streets where there were just apartment houses and nothing else. And these tanks shot against these apartment houses and a considerable part of Budapest became ruins. There were killed children, women, young and old men without distinction . . . there were approximately thirty thousand Hungarians killed by armed forces of Khrushchev. According to official reports two thousand five hundred persons were executed; however, the victims of Khrushchev's secret police are probably higher—twelve thousand persons were deported to the Soviet Union; hundreds of thousands of persons were imprisoned; fifteen thousand were confined to forced labor camps."[1]

It was Khrushchev who gave the order to send Soviet tanks into Budapest. It is Khrushchev who is all-powerful head of the Russia which holds in slave labor camps hundreds of American prisoners, a fact to which former prisoner John Noble has testified from personal experience. It is Khrushchev who is responsible for the orders to Soviet pilots which caused the shooting down of seventeen American airmen over Armenia in late 1958.

It was Khrushchev, who, following the Geneva "summit conference" in 1955 launched the full-scale infiltration of the Middle East.

It was Khrushchev who, following the Geneva Conference in the spring of 1959, kept the Western powers so bemused in Europe by his alternate threats and smiles, his peace offensive, and his Berlin maneuver, that his ally Communist China could thrust its way into India and step up its infiltration of Laos. While Khrushchev offered hope of peace in the West, the Chinese Communists embarked on aggression in the East. It was the same old technique of the carrot and the stick, with Khrushchev holding the carrot and Mao wielding the stick.

Speaking to the workers' conference at Leipzig, East Germany, on March 7, 1959, Khrushchev said: "We are convinced that we shall triumph over capitalism. Not by war, but because we shall prove by deed to all workers of the world the superiority of Communism over capitalism. The working class is in possession of a great truth: the doctrine of Marx and Lenin. And that truth will win the day.

"The question of converting society to Communism is one affecting all the peoples of the world. . . .

"Why do we . . . attach such significance to the German question? Because it is the very core of the problem of war and peace, one of the main sources of international friction and conflict. . . . That is something that must be eliminated. And that is why we stubbornly continue to aim at normalizing the situation in Germany. . . . The most reasonable way out of this situation would be to sign a peace treaty with both German Republics. . . ." [Here Khrushchev is saying that now he will no longer abide by previous agreements to permit free elections in all of Germany and to bring about unity of both Germanies. He has, on his own decision, simply changed the rules—rules to which he and his government agreed in solemn treaties in the past.]

"We are not in favor of just any kind of reunification. The question of reunification must be approached from the point of view of class. . . . If we were to agree to Germany's being reunified on a capitalist basis, comrades, our attitudes would cover us workers with shame. . . . Can we do that? Most certainly not." If Germany is to be reunified, in other words, it must be reunified as a Communist state.

"Comrades, I do ask you not to regard me simply as a representative of my people. Above all I am a Communist, a member of the Communist Party. . . .

"We don't consider the question of frontiers paramount for us Communists and we don't think there can be any conflicts over this matter between socialist countries. . . .

"To us Leninists, the goal of life is the build-up of Communist society. . . . As Marx and Lenin taught us, Communist victory on a world wide scale will result in the abolition of national boundaries. . . .

"Speaking for the future, I consider it most probable that developments in the socialist countries will tend towards consolidating the uniform world system of socialist world economy.

"The question of leveling out the rate of development in those countries where socialism has won through, the question of the gradual extinction of boundaries when every country is Communist, is one of the most important questions in the whole Marxist-Leninist theory. . . .

"We Communists firmly believe in the reality of our plans, and have a perfectly clear concept of how relations between the peoples on this earth must develop. . . .

"Long live Communism. . . ."[2]

This is the real Khrushchev. These words are his own. This is the leader of the Soviet Union, with whom we are associated in the United Nations. The United Nations is a forum for psychological aggression, and a center of intrigue where Communists trap those who dare oppose them, as in the tragedy of Bang-Jensen. It functions as a center of pressure upon us by the Soviet Union, and of pressure applied to us by our allies. They, even more than ourselves, have been successfully indoctrinated by the fear that if we do not give way on every issue to Russia we may be plunged into atomic war.

No illustration can be more pertinent than the crushing of the Hungarian revolution. When the Hungarian people rose against their masters and were victorious, when they controlled Budapest and were backed by all the Hungarian nation, the Soviet Union hesitated. They waited to find out what America would do. But we, under pressure from our allies and trapped by the United Nations climate, did not take the immediate step of recognizing the revolutionary government of Imre Nagy. We gave no assurance of support for the very thing which is the core of our own most historic principle—the right of a people to revolt against tyranny. We delayed in the United Nations for an entire week. We let it become plain that we could not summon up the independent will to support the Hungarians. Meanwhile the United Nations, growing aware that we were not about to intervene in any way, passed "resolutions" and established a "commission." Khrushchev waited no longer. Why should he? Without further delay he struck. He wiped out the Hungarian revolt in a bloody massacre which is still going on.

Hungary proved that the United Nations not only has no physical power or administrative unity to prevent aggression; it also proved that the United Nations has no moral power. For when the puppet Kadar regime, installed with the bayonets of Khrushchev, presented itself to the United Nations for acceptance, it was recognized as the legal government of Hungary. Nobody even walked out, least of all the United States.

Instances from United Nations history abound in similar examples. Except as a forum for Russian pressure, delay and futility are almost the sole and total role of that organization. For example, at the urging of Britain and the United States, the United Nations decided to partition Palestine and create the state of Israel. The Arabs who were dispossessed from their homes and property not unnaturally objected, and the surrounding Arab states attacked the new Israeli nation. Israel won that war and proceeded to expand beyond the borders originally given it by the United Nations. The United Nations has repeatedly passed resolutions telling Israel to return to the original United Nations sponsored borders, and either to compensate or repatriate the Arabs dispossessed. Israel has refused. Then, after Suez, when Israel attacked Egypt while Britain and France tried to occupy the canal zone, the United Nations passed a resolution telling Egypt to allow Israeli ships to pass freely through the newly nationalized canal. Nasser has refused to comply with the United Nations resolution. Since no nation is willing or able to use force to achieve either the United Nations resolutions requiring Israel to return to its borders or the resolution about Israeli shipping, nothing has happened.

The United Nations has more than once shown how easily it can obstruct American action in such a way as to cause loss of American lives. General MacArthur, General Stratemeyer, and General Van Fleet all have testified that they could quickly have won the Korean War if they had been allowed to bomb Chinese bases in Manchuria, make diversionary attacks against the Chinese coast, destroy industrial and transportation targets in China, and use the Chinese Nationalist troops which were offered by Chiang Kai-shek. MacArthur even threatened the Chinese, when they came across the border from Manchuria, that he would smash them unless they retreated. For this he was recalled and humiliated by President Truman. Truman had surrendered to the carefully fostered United Nations climate of fear, and for the first time in history an American President allowed a group of foreign nations to dictate how American troops should fight a war. Therefore Communist China grew stronger and more threatening instead of being defeated and disrupted, and perhaps even overthrown.

What is the attitude of the United Nations when, instead of the interests of the United States or one of the countries of the free world, Soviet interests are at stake? In 1959 a group of Kalmuks, people of Central Asian ancestry with ties to the people of Tibet, organized a march from Farmingdale, Long Island, to the United Nations headquarters in New York. Their purpose was to protest the brutal aggression of Red China against

Tibet. They were met at the United Nations by a wall of cold silence. Andrew Cordier, Hammarskjold's American assistant whom we have discussed before, was at that time acting for the Secretary General, who was in Moscow. Cordier refused to see the Kalmuks. He refused to permit any pictures to be taken inside the United Nations. He prevented the Kalmuks from making any demonstration. Why? Perhaps it was because Cordier remembered that in July 1958, after a demonstration by Hungarians in New York against the Russians, Khrushchev threatened to pull the Soviet Union out of the United Nations if any more demonstrations were permitted. This threat apparently frightened the United Nations Secretariat in much the same way as Khrushchev's threat to go home if Americans didn't stop insulting him frightened Ambassador Lodge into appealing for an end to the heckling. One hard word from Khrushchev and the world drops on its knees.

Judge Robert Morris of New Jersey, former chief counsel of the Senate Internal Security Committee, commented, "In this way he [Cordier] suppressed human protests from people who have no other means to aid their brothers in their cries of death."[3]

In the words of an editorial written at that time, "most Americans have thought that the United Nations was formed to protect the liberty and the independence of all peoples and nations and give heed to protest against aggression and oppression. Instead it appears that the United Nations has become an instrument to protect

Communist aggressors from criticism, and to silence the voices crying for freedom in the world."

To anyone who observes the facts, the gap between the myth about the United Nations and the real United Nations is almost incredible. The United Nations, reputed the great association for peace, is actually an instrument of Soviet penetration and domination. Not only does the Soviet Union dominate the Security Council with its veto and the General Assembly by its aggressive policy, but it even seems that its agents may be on their way to controlling the entire apparatus of the United Nations Secretariat. We have seen how powerful Soviet influence must have been over the Secretariat in the case of Povl Bang-Jensen. There are other signs.

In October 1959 Ambassador Lodge protested to the United Nations Secretariat against the ending of daily United Nations broadcasts to Hungary. He said the decision was "unacceptable." But protest is the limit of Lodge's power. He has no control over what the Secretariat does. The United Nations Office of Public Information (OPI) is wholly under the control of Hammarskjold, who appoints the top executives.

And who are these top executives? In an article in a recent periodical, R. E. Troper describes what may be at least one powerful source of Soviet influence in the Secretariat.[4] A man named Boris Karpov is a principal officer of OPI, and his assistant is Boris N. Ivanov, former press chief of the Soviet delegation. In September 1958, a six-man committee appointed by Hammarskjold to recommend reorganization of OPI issued a report. One of the most important members of this committee of six was Anatoly Dobrynin of the Soviet Union, Undersecretary for Political and Security Council Affairs, *head of the United Nations Security police and custodian of all diplomatic documents including secret information involving the safety of refugees!* Another member was A. F. Sokirkin, USSR. The possibilities of this combination are practically endless.

What did the report on OPI recommend? It recommended that the free press covering the United Nations be expelled as United Nations correspondents and that they be replaced by United Nations employees. It recommended a new role for OPI: "The problem is to find ways and means of getting the few documents through to the few people who are most keenly interested. This is another way of saying that the general approach [that is, permitting United Nations correspondents freely to report all the news from the United Nations] is a waste of time. It comes down to a public relations job rather than a public information job. . . . With this new orientation would arise a new conception of the Office of Public Information Headquarters as a strong center for guiding, coordinating and planning the over-all work."[5] Under Karpov and Ivanov, of course.

United Nations correspondents, naturally, objected strenuously to the disappearance of free reporting. At least temporarily, Hammarskjold dropped this part of the OPI plan. Troper in his article suggests that a bargain may have been made by correspondents, who may have said that they would go easy on the Bang-Jensen case if they could keep their accreditation. Whether this is true or not I do not know. But certainly they did go easy on the Bang-Jensen case. We at the *Star* had to do our own investigating, and until Bang-Jensen died, the case got a press coverage whose meagerness seems entirely abnormal.

In any event, OPI now has plans to set up Information Agencies in each of the eighty-two countries represented in the United Nations. They would be, of course, public relations agencies for the United Nations, supervised and dominated by the Soviet officials in New York like Karpov and Ivanov. Therefore, we have here centered in our own country, an agency of supposedly accurate information, but dominated by pro-Communist officials, one third of whose salaries and expenses are paid for by the United States taxpayer. Can anyone doubt that a function of this agency will be to spread propaganda satisfactory to Russia? Nevertheless, Dag Hammarskjold, who is ultimately responsible for OPI, welcomes this "bold new revision of the United Nations press services" and said that he looked forward to the time when United Nations Information Agencies around the world will create a sense "of togetherness of the people of the United Nations."

No one is a more ardent public spokesman on behalf of the United Nations than our own ambassador. However, at the end of the United Nations 1958 session

Lodge stated that failures of the session were due to "the intransigent and contentious attitude of the Soviet Union." He is admitting that the Soviet Union can and does dominate the United Nations. He is saying that no constructive action can be taken without Soviet approval.

Furthermore, when Lodge was asked why the United States took no action while the Hungarian revolt was being crushed, he replied that "we took no action" because of "the apparent impossibility of getting a two thirds majority."[6] Actually, this means two things. One is that two thirds of the United Nations will not stand with the United States in case of aggression against either us or another country. The other is that the American government will not even try to oppose such aggressions unless we can get a two thirds majority, which Lodge admits we cannot get.

Therefore, for the United States to limit its action to measures to be taken within the framework of the United Nations means in effect to put America and the free world at the mercy of the Soviet Union. Any United Nations decision can be vetoed by the Soviet Union in the Security Council. Any decision of the General Assembly is at the mercy of the Soviet Union and the Afro-Asian bloc of pro-Soviet or neutral nations. We can obviously never be sure of a two thirds majority supporting us in the Assembly. In fact, in one specific case, the Assembly majority quite easily overturned the American position.

Remember Lebanon? When the Iraqi coup of Kassem occurred in July 1958, President Eisenhower acted without United Nations sanction and sent U.S. Marines to Lebanon. But then he asked United Nations delegate Henry Cabot Lodge to get United Nations approval of the American action, as Truman did in Korea. It was obvious the Security Council would not approve it, for this time the Soviet delegate was in his seat, instead of having walked out as he had during the Korean crisis. The veto was there.

Lodge, therefore, tried to line up United Nations support for the United States in the General Assembly. What happened? Hammarskjold told Lodge that the United Nations observation team in Lebanon was quite capable of taking care of the situation and that this United Nations team would not cooperate with the United States! Japan and Sweden openly criticized the American action. Even Latin American delegates stayed silent. The Soviet Union began lining up support by playing on everybody's fear of war. But *note that the Soviet Union backed quickly away from its threat of intervention once the American invasion started.*

To avoid getting into an Assembly debate in which the United States would clearly take a verbal beating and perhaps be voted down, Lodge tried to get a United Nations force established to take the place of the Marines. The Soviet Union threatened a veto. Britain and France advised the United States this time to ignore the United Nations and go ahead on its own. But Lodge was determined to get the "moral support" of the United Nations. Instead of giving it, however, a majority decided to call a special session to debate the Middle East. The result was no United Nations support for American action, and a mildly critical resolution instead.

It is very important to remember what happened in Lebanon. The United States felt compelled to take direct action. The action was completed. *The Soviet Union did nothing.* Russia had its turn at silence in the game of terror of atomic war. For once Khrushchev had to sit with hands quietly folded.

There are endless illustrations which in today's circumstances indicate the effectiveness of American action, compared with the hopelessness of attempted action through the United Nations. What happened in Korea? There the United States acted swiftly, and I believe rightly, in meeting with force aggression from Communist North Korea. Without asking anybody's permission, President Truman ordered American troops into action. Then he made his fatal mistake. He asked that the United Nations take over management of the action and assume responsibility for its outcome. The United Nations did so. But no other nation joined in the fighting in Korea except small token forces from close allies of the United States like Britain, France, and Turkey. The money, arms, and men came chiefly from the United States. The direction, however, came from the United Nations, in which Communists sat as members. And we know the tragic stalemate which resulted.

Right after World War II the United Nations appointed a commission to investigate Communist aggression in Greece. The Soviet Union, Yugoslavia, and Bulgaria, all Communist states, ignored the commission. How was Greece saved? By unilateral American military and economic action under the Truman Doctrine. If the United States had not acted alone, Greece would have lost to the revolutionary forces supported by the Communists, and Greece would today be thrusting a Communist tentacle into the Mediterranean.

Not long after the incident of Greece came Kashmir. India and Pakistan were feuding over control of this predominantly Moslem state. Predominantly Hindu India occupied predominantly Moslem Kashmir with troops. A United Nations commission was established to carry out a plebiscite, so the citizens of Kashmir could vote and decide whether to join India or Pakistan. But Indian troops jailed supporters of the plebiscite in Kashmir and prevented any settlement. That is still the situation in Kashmir ten years later. The United Nations failed because it has neither the unity nor the power to succeed without the direct action of a strong power like the United States.

Was Tibet saved by the United Nations? It was difficult enough in 1959 even to persuade the members to debate the question, much less act at the time of the murder of this small country.

United Nations apologists give the United Nations credit for stopping the Soviet attempt to take over Azerbaijan in Iran right after the war. But until the United States moved to intervene in Iran, there was no possibility of United Nations action. The only credit the United Nations can take in regard to present conditions in Korea is responsibility for its failure to achieve what the United Nations resolved it should achieve, free elections and self-government. Nevertheless deluded people in this country still keep proposing that the United Nations be given the responsibility of protecting areas like Berlin and Formosa from aggression. This is simply a formula for the capture of both places by the Communists. All experience with the United Nations proves it.

It is a dangerous world when so many of its people persist in believing what experience proves false. Those who keep saying we should strengthen the United Nations and give it more, not less, responsibility remind me of a story I heard while I was in Berlin in September 1959. It seems there was a German professor named Baer in Koenigsberg who said, "It is true that all men are mortal. But this does not necessarily mean that all men must die. It means only that up to this date all men have died." The obvious question then was asked. "Is Professor Baer still alive?" The reply is, "No, he died before he could prove his theory."

It seems that there are still many people in the world like Professor Baer who are willing to see freedom die for the sake of a theory which is demonstrably false, yet the theory stubbornly goes on, developing its own life and its own consistencies, which have nothing to do with fact. If circumstances or an upsurge of American will does not stop its growth, the "togetherness" theory of the United Nations could well continue until the day when it would develop into something like a real life version of *1984's* Ministry of Love.

When the United States turns over to the United Nations responsibilities which could have been fulfilled by the United States alone, but cannot be fulfilled through the United Nations, then the United States is committing an immoral action. It is abandoning the first principle of conduct of free nations—namely, that the first duty of every nation is self-preservation for the sake of its citizens. A nation is constituted by its people for their own protection and preservation.

When the United States abdicates responsibility for making a decision which affects the interests not only of its own people but of the people of other free nations and the millions within the enslaved nations, the cause of "good faith" and "justice" is weakened at its very base. American abdication of the responsibilities it turns over to the United Nations is in fact a new kind of isolationism. It is irresponsibility carried to the highest possible peak. For many years the new isolationists led by such distinguished diplomats as Dean Acheson declared with assurance and conviction, "The United Nations is the cornerstone of American foreign policy." Yet even Dean Acheson now rejects this view. Writing in the fall 1959 issue of *Orbis,* a quarterly journal of world affairs published by the Foreign Policy Research Institute of the University of Pennsylvania, Acheson says: "This, then is the general picture of the world as it is unfolding in the last half of the twentieth century. There is a strong tendency to escape from it—to believe that this can somehow be avoided through the United Nations. This is impossible. . . . When the late Senator Vandenberg called the General Assembly of the United Nations 'the town meeting of the world' he was being poetic. It has none of the qualities of the town meeting. . . . The United Nations has no power, and it will not acquire any power. . . . The United Nations insofar as it believes that by its votes and by its debates it is accomplishing anything could not be more mistaken. In fact, it can be harmful."

Dean Acheson is not alone in recognizing the powerlessness of the United Nations in dealing with aggression. Sir Leslie Munroe, British delegate to the United Nations, recently said much the same thing: "If Laos becomes the victim of aggression, it hardly seems likely that the United Nations will save her, given the fact that the world organization has no standby force, which even by its simple presence might deter military activity. It will be only SEATO, or more probably its principal party, the United States, that can or will come to the aid of this distressed country. In other words, the chief bulwark of endangered states today is not the United Nations but either a great power or a regional organization."[6]

Men like Acheson and Munroe see this fact clearly, now. But how long before all the people who in years past followed such leaders into these fatal patterns will also be able to see?

The new isolationism, which is the real meaning of our surrender of responsibility to the United Nations, has been caused by two psychological factors: first, the fear that if the United States stands alone for the right, and for peace and freedom and justice in the world, we will not win, and we may plunge the entire globe into atomic war; second, the fatal confidence in the United Nations, which is not what it appears to be, but the very opposite. A friend not long ago wrote an editorial which to me seemed to get at the heart of the matter. I hope I may be forgiven if I use his words instead of my own. He described our present course as "suicide of our national soul."

What evoked the phrase was a set of circumstances which developed as follows: In reaction to an editorial trying to describe to the public the true meaning of turning over funds and American responsibilities to the United Nations, an angry reader sent in the quotation from John Donne with which I began this chapter, "No man is an island." My friend[8] wrote in reply: "Every man is an island in a sea of humanity. And every man—though he may constantly surround himself with companions—must live some part of his life alone. Every man must live some part of his life in the inner recesses of his mind and soul, where none but he and his Maker may go.

"Military people have sayings about the loneliness of command. It is not a physical loneliness, but a loneliness of mind which is known in those moments when decisions must be made and no part of the responsibility can be passed away to any other human, decisions on which may hang the lives of men or the fate of a nation. . . . He can turn to no other human to share the burden. Any man who has never known this loneliness of decision is a man who has never taken command of his own soul.

"It is so with nations also. A nation lives among other nations as a man lives among other men. But there come moments when a nation must make its own decisions in the loneliness of its own soul and conscience. A nation, for better or worse, does have a soul and a conscience. In such a lonely hour the decision to send troops to Lebanon was made. The decision . . . to withdraw the troops . . . similarly was made by the United States alone. The United Nations is not going to make decisions for us in any way which will lift from our shoulders the responsibility for them.

"If we think that the United States can become but one faceless nation among other faceless nations, living always together and never alone, we merely delude ourselves. . . .

"The peril of the United Nations for America is that we might try to leave the making of our decisions to it. . . . We as a nation have principles to uphold. We have standards to live by. We have the freedom and the dignity of man to cherish. When these principles and standards, freedom and the other things we cherish are at stake, we alone must make our decisions according to our principles. Anything less is suicide of our national soul."

CHAPTER X

"THE SPIRIT THAT MOVES HUMANITY"

The resemblances between our own period and eras of decline in classical antiquity are startling and often prophetic. One of our greatest modern scholars in the field of Greek history and literature wrote last year: "Is it rational that now when the young people may have to face problems harder than we face, is it reasonable that with the atomic age before them, at this time we are giving up the study of how the Greeks and Romans prevailed magnificently in a barbaric world; the study, too, of how that triumph ended, how a slackness and softness finally came over them to their ruin? In the end more than they wanted freedom, they wanted security, a comfortable life, and they lost all—security, comfort, and freedom. . . .

"Cicero said, 'To be ignorant of the past is to remain a

child.' Santayana said, 'A nation that does not know history is fated to repeat it.' . . . The first nation in the world to be free sends a ringing call down through the centuries to all who would be free. Greece rose to the heights, not because she was big, she was very small; not because she was rich, she was very poor; not even because she was so wonderfully gifted. So doubtless were others in the ancient world who have gone their way, leaving little for us. She rose because there was in the Greeks the greatest spirit that moves in humanity, *the spirit that sets men free.*"[1]

For centuries that spirit lived in us. Brissot de Warville wrote of the Americans in 1791, "No danger, no distance, no obstacles detain them." Sixty years later Charles Mackay said, "The real motto of their country is 'go ahead.' " The nineteenth-century Swedish novelist Frederika Bremer, commenting on the tendency of the average American to boast, replied, "Why not? He is a man who can rely on himself; and he is a citizen of a great nation designed to be the greatest on the face of the earth."

We were. Are we still? We can be.

But only if freedom is our first goal. Only if we set our own liberty above all other considerations, in domestic affairs and in foreign affairs. The time is past when we can separate the two. We live or we die as a nation among nations, as part of all civilization, as a portion of all free men. In this sense, no man indeed is an island. Our own life or death at home and abroad depends on our vitality in the cause of human liberty, and the cause of human liberty to a great extent depends on our vitality. And unless we live by the principles embodied in our own Declaration of Independence, which says that all men are endowed by their Creator with certain unalienable rights, and to secure these rights governments are instituted among men, we will not live long.

Our peril has come upon us so gradually, it has mounted so slowly, with such concealment, so insidiously, with warm promises of security, with the true danger so hidden by the apathy and indifference flowing from our own weakened will, that we have scarcely been aware of it. A reader once wrote me a letter in which he told the story of a Wyoming farmer and a frog. The farmer discovered that you can throw a frog right into boiling water and it will not inflict any injury. Any frog has the sense to jump out of the boiling water so quickly that he is not harmed. However, the farmer also discovered that if you put the frog into comfortable luke-warm water and then slowly heat the water until to comes to a boil, you can cook the frog to a turn.

As the writer of the letter put it, "He, like the American people, can be lulled into such a sense of security that he can be cooked."

The letter writer was a man of discernment. Security seems to be what most Americans want above all else. Perhaps this is not surprising. Americans, like the Greeks two thousand years ago, have built a great and splendid civilization. We have achieved liberty. We have achieved a way of life such as the world has never seen. The Greeks "wanted security, a comfortable life" more than they wanted freedom, and they therefore went unheedingly to their destruction. Will we?

Whatever the current Communist line, it is intended to destroy us. Are the Communists multiplying their armies? It is because they intend to destroy us. Are they diminishing their armies and urging mutual disarmament? It is because they believe that at present the task of destroying us will be easier in a world disarmed, even if they have to disarm themselves to some degree. The aim never varies, only the means change to suit the circumstances. Our destruction is their purpose. They can have no other, for our survival means their doom. As long as any portion of the globe is inhabited by free men, the world's enslaved peoples will sooner or later lift their heads, and seeing that there are somewhere other men who wear no chains, they will stir restlessly in their bonds. The world cannot live in peace half slave and half free. The Soviet system and our free system cannot exist indefinitely side by side. The Communists know this and have always known it, though we are coming to the realization slowly and with the greatest reluctance. Are we to seek "peace" with them, when it means total loss of freedom for ourselves and for others? Are we to seek security for ourselves by selling the liberties of those who, following our example, seek to throw off the shackles of the past and emerge into the light of national independence and personal freedom?

If we do, we will, like Rome and Greece, fall before an opponent far less powerful, far less intelligent, far less capable than we.

We must rediscover the will to freedom. Then we must defend and expand that will. To be free is to take risks. To be free is to live in the presence of danger without fearing it.

So what do we do, if we believe that American freedom, our freedom, is worth any sacrifice and any hardship? In 1862, Abraham Lincoln wrote in a letter to Horace Greeley: "My paramount object in this struggle is to save the Union, and not either to save or to destroy slavery.

"If I could save the Union without freeing any slave, I would do it; if I could do it by freeing all slaves, I would do that; and if I could save it by freeing some and leaving others alone, I would also do that.

"What I do about slavery and the colored race, I do because I believe it helps save the Union; and what I forbear, I forbear because I do not believe it would help save the Union. . . .

"I shall try to correct errors when shown to be errors, and I shall adopt new views as fast as they shall appear to be true views.

"I have here stated my purpose according to my official duty, and I intend no modification of my oft expressed personal wish that all men everywhere could be free."[2]

This is a letter which after the Civil War was sometimes quoted in the South to show that Lincoln was not an idealist, that he cared nothing for freeing the slaves, and that his purposes were solely political and economic. In precisely the same spirit, people who today point out that self-preservation is the first duty of nations (as Washington knew, as all intelligent statesmen have always known) are accused of caring nothing for that principle of sovereign powers which enjoins faith and justice. We know from the text of other Lincoln documents what the slavery issue meant to him. The belief that he acted from political and economic motives arose only from the prejudice and bitterness left behind by the War between the States. The accusation was false. What Lincoln's letter truly signified was simply the paramount fact that if the nation were ruptured asunder, the problem of slavery or freedom in America would become academic, for America would have ceased to exist. If America today does not effectively preserve first of all her own existence, she will strike the cause of world freedom the greatest possible blow. That she must think first of her own self-preservation before she turns to other nations is evident. If America herself is destroyed, what aid can she give to others?

So the primary goal of American foreign policy must be the preservation and strengthening of the United States. Other goals are secondary and subservient to that. If we make alliances they must be made with that end in view. If we work in the United Nations, that goal must be paramount. We cannot save the world alone. We can, however, save ourselves. And if we do that, perhaps the world can save itself, and we may help effectively toward that end.

This is the sound view. This is the practical view. This

is the ethical view. In its light we can easily see which acts of our government are well-advised and which are foolish, which are workable, and which will not work. Let us take some examples: In dealing with the Middle East what should American policy be? It should be American. "*All men* are endowed by their Creator with certain unalienable rights." That means Egyptians, Algerians, Syrians, Lebanese, and Israelis too. When they seek to establish for themselves these unalienable rights, should we seek to deny them? On the contrary, we must sympathize, encourage, and assist them. In dealing with the so-called "backward nations" of the world we should keep to our true character, which once made us the most respected and honored and loved nation in the world.

American charitable, religious, and educational organizations have for scores of years been sending technical and financial aid to institutions and organizations in other countries. Missionaries and teachers have gone forth to brave danger and sickness to help less fortunate people than we. This is the kind of "foreign aid" for which our people have become loved and honored.

When disaster has struck in foreign lands, as it did in Japan in the fall of 1959 after a typhoon killed thousands, the American military and civilian authorities went quickly to the aid of the stricken people with planes and shelter and food. This is the kind of humane spirit that Americans have always shown toward others. Remember, it was an American, Herbert Hoover, who fed both Belgians and Russians after the ravages of World War I with the help of both private and government organizations. We should encourage and increase this kind of unselfish help to others.

The technical aid programs of American government in foreign countries are good programs. They are run by technicians who know their business and who can in small ways accomplish things that will not only win friends for this country, but help others win for themselves a better life and more freedom to live it. But technical aid to backward countries is only a tiny percentage of our foreign aid budget, about $160,000,000. This we should continue and increase. But we must stop this foolish and dangerous interference in the lives of peoples, as we have done, for example, with the Laotians and Lebanese and Turks.

In 1957 I spent an evening in the Cairo home of Ambassador Abdul Khalek Hassouna, Secretary General of the Arab League. I asked him what the Arabs wanted from the United States. Was it aid? Was it money? Was it arms? His answer was revealing, "We would like to see the United States act toward us as she used to act," he said. "The Arab people have always loved and respected Americans when you sent your missionaries, your educators, your philanthropists and your businessmen here. But when you take political sides with the British or French, we do not like that. . . . Whenever the United States bases its policies toward us on the principles of your Declaration of Independence, when you act solely in your own American interests according to what is

174

right, as President Eisenhower did when he opposed the British and French in their attack on Suez, we always will be your friend. America never can be challenged successfully by any nation when you act according to your American principles. . . ."

When United States foreign policy is truly our own it succeeds. When it is partly American and partly British or French it fails.

Another foreign statesman, Carlos Romulo of the Philippines, put it this way: "America will never be wrong if, whenever she is faced by this unhappy choice [of supporting anti-colonial movements] she elects not to sacrifice principle for expediency. This is a hard road to follow, since America needs her European allies to counter the threat of Soviet power. . . . But America cannot tolerate or underwrite such ruinous enterprises [as the attack on Suez] and expect these allies to remain strong. Nor can she retain the confidence of the peoples struggling to be free."[3]

Elmo Hutchinson, whom I met in Cairo and traveled with in Lebanon and Jordan in 1957, is the Middle East Director of the American Friends of the Middle East. A former commander in the navy, he is author of *The Violent Truce,* a book on Arab-Israeli clashes. Writing from Cairo in a letter predicting the Kassem coup in Iraq almost to the day, he said, "Let's forget about this man Nasser for a while and think of America in our dealings. We will find that nationalism, even eventual Arab federation [the idea of federation, like the idea of popular revolt, is an American concept] matches up with our principles and beliefs. If we look for ourselves we will also find that neutralism on the part of the Arabs offers no real dangers, as the basic roots of culture and economy spread to the West. By aligning ourselves with the Arab desire for self-identity on the stage of world politics, we will give encouragement to those who champion nationalism and will remove from them the feeling that they have no room in which to maneuver. Until we change our policy, the Arab is hard pressed to turn his back on his only source of military and economic aid. The West dreams too loudly of redividing and ruling the Middle East."[4]

When dealing with Europe, which by division, historic enmities, and fratricidal wars has laid itself open to invasion by the new Soviet colossus, should we assume their burdens and involve ourselves in their quarrels? No. If they seek what we have won, let us help them. If they are struggling for independence from Soviet conquest by unity and free association, by economic and political and military cooperation, we should encourage and aid them. But never should we permit the power of decision as to what we shall do pass into their hands. We have twice fought to save Europe, and twice afterwards seen the rise of "even worse perils than we have surmounted." American freedom is not dependent on European freedom, though we must admit that the loss of Europe to Communism would bring about terrible danger to us.

But Europe will not stay free if Europe does not want to stay free, no matter how we might arm, guard, or cajole her. If the nations of Europe want liberty and independence, we must help. But we cannot tie ourselves to Europe by bonds which endanger our own national survival, nor can we tie ourselves to Israel, or India, or the Arab nations, or even little Laos.

Toward the Soviet Union we should adopt a policy based on our true character. We should assert our historic and enduring wish "that all men everywhere could be free." We should make it clear to the Soviet leaders that we will encourage and assist any country that seeks to throw off Communist bondage, whether it be China, Tibet, or East Germany. The Communists tell us they intend to "bury" us. We should reply that we expect to see them buried, and freedom arise in Russia as well as in Eastern Europe and Asia.

We should put the Soviet Union on the defensive with clear notice that we intend to *win* the cold war, and that at the same time we have the military power to prevent a hot war. The Soviet Union, by its propaganda and threats, has pushed us into accepting the false proposition that if we do not seek peace at all costs by mutual agreement, we will get atomic war that can destroy the world. That is nonsense. The Kremlin does not accept that proposition. While we talk, they move into Hungary, or Tibet, or Vietnam, or Korea. They wage Communism while we sit idle. Instead we should be waging freedom. In the

177

instances when we have waged freedom, it has been the Soviet Union which has had to sit idle, and we who have advanced.

As long as we seek "peace" in the Soviet sense more than we seek freedom and liberty, we will remain on the defensive, and the Communists will keep on winning. If we wanted that sort of peace at Quemoy, we could have had it at the price of surrender. We can have peace in Berlin at the price of surrender. We can end the whole cold war at the price of surrender.

There is only one reason for carrying on the cold war. That is to preserve our liberty and extend all human liberty. If our liberty is not important, we should quit now and avoid further dangers. If liberty is important, nothing should deter us. Liberty for the United States must be our first aim. Liberty for all others who seek it, who will fight for it, who will dare revolt as the Algerians dare it, who will dare resistance as Turkey and South Korea dare it, who will risk all for liberty, as the Hungarians did—this should be our second and concomitant line of action. Our foreign policy must be based on this concept. Until it is, we will not even begin to succeed.

Why has the former colonial world turned against the United States since World War II? Dorothy Thompson, whose shrewdness and prophetic intuition have become almost legendary, has written: "Their natural protector was the United States, born in an anti-colonial revolution, and anti-colonial in its grass roots spirit ever since, despite various lapses. In Asia, Africa, and the Near East, 'America' was synonymous with personal liberty and national freedom and independence. The torch that the socialist camp is now so successfully carrying was first raised by us, and was right at hand. In raising it we could have turned the renascent old nations away from Russia and Communism, toward independence and self fulfillment.

"Why did we not do so? . . .

"Because we ourselves have not been free. Through military alliances, mutual aid programs, support of Zionist ambitions, and what not, we have entangled ourselves in the problems of dissolving colonial empires, incurred the displeasure of our European allies and the disappointment of the new Eastern nations that amounts to the hatred of frustrated love. . . . Our relations with other countries, often contradictory, have been influenced by powerful penetrations in behalf of interests other than our own."[5]

That is why American foreign policy has failed you. It is no longer American. It no longer holds to our abiding principles. It no longer expresses what *you* are.

Or does it?

APPENDIX A

President Washington's Address to the People of the
United States Intimating His Resolution of Retiring
from Public Service
1796

Friends and Fellow-Citizens, the period for a new election of a Citizen to administer the executive government
of the United States, being not far distant, and the time
actually arrived, when your thoughts must be employed
in designating the person, who is to be cloathed with
that important trust, it appears to me proper, especially
as it may conduce to a more distinct expression of the
public voice, that I should now apprise you of the resolution I have formed, to decline being considered among
the number of those, out of whom a choice is to be made.

I beg you, at the same time, to do me the justice to be
assured, that this resolution has not been taken, without
a strict regard to all the considerations appertaining to
the relation, which binds a dutiful citizen to his country;
and that in withdrawing the tender of service which silence in my situation might imply, I am influenced by no

diminution of zeal for your future interest; no deficiency of grateful respect for your past kindness; but am supported by a full conviction that the step is compatible with both.

The acceptance of, and continuance hitherto in the office to which your suffrages have twice called me, have been a uniform sacrifice of inclination to the opinion of duty, and to a deference for what appeared to be your desire. I constantly hoped, that it would have been much earlier in my power, consistently with motives, which I was not at liberty to disregard, to return to that retirement, from which I had been reluctantly drawn. The strength of my inclination to do this, previous to the last election, had even led to the preparation of an address to declare it to you; but mature reflection on the then perplexed and critical posture of our affairs with foreign nations, and the unanimous advice of persons entitled to my confidence, impelled me to abandon the idea.

I rejoice, that the state of your concerns, external as well as internal, no longer renders the pursuit of inclination incompatible with the sentiment of duty, or propriety; and am persuaded whatever partiality may be retained for my services, that in the present circumstances of our country, you will not disapprove my determination to retire.

The impressions with which I first undertook the arduous trust, were explained on the proper occasion. In the discharge of this trust, I will only say, that I have with good intentions, contributed towards the organization and administration of the government, the best exertions of which a very fallible judgment was capable. Not unconscious, in the out set, of the inferiority of my qualifications, experience in my own eyes, perhaps still more in the eyes of others, has strengthened the motives to diffidence of myself; and every day the encreasing weight of years admonishes me more and more, that the shade of retirement is as necessary to me as it will be welcome. Satisfied that if any circumstances have given peculiar value to my services, they were temporary, I have the consolation to believe, that while choice and prudence invite me to quit the political scene, patriotism does not forbid it.

In looking forward to the moment, which is intended to terminate the career of my public life, my feelings do not permit me to suspend the deep acknowledgment of that debt of gratitude which I owe to my beloved country, for the many honours it has conferred upon me; still more for the steadfast confidence with which it has supported me; and for the opportunities I have thence enjoyed of manifesting my inviolable attachment, by services faithful and persevering, though in usefulness unequal to my zeal. If benefits have resulted to our country from these services, let it always be remembered to your praise, and as an instructive example in our annals, that under circumstances in which the passions, agitated in every direction, were liable to mislead, amidst appearances sometimes dubious,—vicissitudes of fortune often discouraging,—in situations in which not unfrequently want of success has countenanced the spirit of criticism—the constancy of your support was the essential prop of the efforts, and a guarantee of the plans by which they were effected.—Profoundly penetrated with this idea, I shall carry it with me to my grave, as a strong incitement to unceasing vows that Heaven may continue to you the choicest tokens of its beneficence—that your union and brotherly affection may be perpetual—that the free constitution, which is the work of your hands, may be sacredly maintained—that its administration in every department may be stamped with wisdom and virtue—that, in fine, the happiness of the people of these States, under the auspices of liberty, may be made complete, by so careful a preservation and so prudent a use of this blessing as will acquire to them the glory of recommending it to the applause, the affection and adoption of every nation which is yet a stranger to it.

Here, perhaps, I ought to stop. But a solicitude for your welfare, which cannot end but with my life, and the apprehension of danger, natural to that solicitude, urge me on an occasion like the present, to offer to your solemn contemplation, and to recommend to your frequent review, some sentiments; which are the result of much reflection, of no inconsiderable observation, and which appear to me all-important to the permanency of your felicity as a People. These will be offered to you with the more freedom, as you can only see in them the disinterested warnings of a parting friend, who can possibly have no personal motive to bias his counsel. Nor can I forget, as an encouragement to it, your indulgent reception of my sentiments on a former and not dissimilar occasion.

Interwoven as is the love of liberty with every ligament of your hearts, no recommendation of mine is necessary to fortify or confirm the attachment.

The unity of Government which constitutes you one people, is also now dear to you. It is justly so; for it is a main pillar in the edifice of your real independence, the support of your tranquility at home, your peace abroad; of your safety; of your prosperity; of that very Liberty which you so highly prize. But as it is easy to foresee, that from different causes and from different quarters, much pains will be taken, many artifices employed to weaken in your minds the conviction of this truth; as this is the point in your political fortress against which the batteries of internal and external enemies will be most constantly and actively (though often covertly and insidiously) directed, it is of infinite moment, that you should properly estimate the immense value of your national Union, to your collective and individual happiness; that you should cherish a cordial habitual and immovable attachment to it; accustoming yourselves to think and speak of it as of the Palladium of your political safety and prosperity; watching for its preservation with jealous anxiety; discountenancing whatever may suggest even a suspicion that it can in any event be abandoned; and indignantly frowning upon the first dawning of every attempt to alienate any portion of our country from the rest, or to enfeeble the sacred ties which now link together the various parts.

For this you have every inducement of sympathy and interest. Citizens by birth or choice, of a common country, that country has a right to concentrate your affections. The name of AMERICAN, which belongs to you, in your national capacity, must always exalt the just pride of Patriotism, more than any appellation derived from local discriminations. With slight shades of difference, you have the same religion, manners, habits and political principles. You have in a common cause fought and triumphed together; the Independence and Liberty you possess are the work of joint councils, and joint efforts, of common dangers, sufferings and successes.

But these considerations, however powerfully they address themselves to your sensibility, are greatly outweighed by those which apply more immediately to your interest.—Here every portion of our country finds the most commanding motives for carefully guarding and preserving the Union of the whole.

The *North*, in an unrestrained intercourse with the *South*, protected by the equal laws of a common government, finds in the productions of the latter, great additional resources of maritime and commercial enterprise and precious materials of manufacturing industry.—The *South* in the same intercourse, benefitting by the Agency of the *North*, sees its agriculture grow and its commerce expand. Turning partly into its own channels the seamen of the *North*, it finds its particular navigation invigorated;—and while it contributes, in different ways, to nourish and increase the general mass of the national navigation, it looks forward to the protection of a maritime strength, to which itself is unequally adapted.—The *East*, in a like intercourse with the *West*, already finds, and in the progressive improvement of interior communications, by land and water, will more and more find a valuable vent for the commodities which it brings from abroad, or manufactures at home.—The *West* derives from the *East*, supplies requisite to its growth and comfort—and what is perhaps of still greater consequence, it must of necessity owe the *secure* enjoyment of indispensible *outlets* for its own productions to the weight, influence, and the future maritime strength of the Atlantic side of the Union, directed by an indissoluble community of interest as *one nation*.—Any other tenure by which the *West* can hold this essential advantage, whether derived from its own separate strength, or from an apostate and unnatural connection with any foreign power, must be intrinsically precarious.

While then every part of our country thus feels an immediate and particular interest in Union, all the parts combined cannot fail to find in the united mass of means and efforts greater strength, greater resource, proportionably greater security from external danger, a less frequent interruption of their peace by foreign nations;—and what is of inestimable value! they must derive from Union an exemption from those broils and wars between themselves, which so frequently afflict neighbouring countries, not tied together by the same government; which their own rivalships alone would be sufficient to produce, but which opposite foreign alliances, attachments and intrigues would stimulate and imbitter.— Hence likewise they will avoid the necessity of those overgrown military establishments, which under any form of government are inauspicious to liberty, and which are to be regarded as particularly hostile to Republican Liberty; in this sense it is, that your Union ought to be considered as a main prop of your liberty, and that the love of the one ought to endear to you the preservation of the other.

These considerations speak a persuasive language to every reflecting and virtuous mind, and exhibit the continuance of the UNION as a primary object of patriotic desire.—Is there a doubt, whether a common government can embrace so large a sphere?—Let experience solve it. To listen to mere speculation in such a case were criminal. We are authorized to hope that a proper organization of the whole, with the auxiliary agency of governments for the respective subdivisions, will afford a happy issue to the experiment. 'Tis well worth a fair and full experiment. With such powerful and obvious motives to Union, affecting all parts of our country, while experience shall not have demonstrated its impracticability, there will always be reason to distrust the patriotism of those, who in any quarter may endeavour to weaken its bands.

In contemplating the causes which may disturb our

Union, it occurs as matter of serious concern, that any ground should have been furnished for characterising parties by *Geographical* discriminations—*Northern* and *Southern*—*Atlantic* and *Western;* whence designing men may endeavour to excite a belief that there is a real difference of local interests and views. One of the expedients of party to acquire influence, within particular districts, is to misrepresent the opinions and aims of other districts. You cannot shield yourselves too much against the jealousies and heart burnings which spring from these misrepresentations: they tend to render alien to each other those who ought to be bound together by fraternal affection. The inhabitants of our western country have lately had a useful lesson on this head: they have seen in the negociation by the Executive, and in the unanimous ratification by the Senate, of the treaty with Spain, and in the universal satisfaction at that event, throughout the United States, a decisive proof how unfounded were the suspicions propagated among them of the policy in the General Goverment and in the Atlantic States unfriendly to their interests in regard of the Mississippi: they have been witnesses to the formation of two treaties, that with Great Britain and that with Spain, which secure to them every thing they could desire, in respect to our foreign relations, towards confirming their prosperity. Will it not be their wisdom to rely for the preservation of these advantages on the Union by which they were procured? Will they not henceforth be deaf to those advisers, if such there are, who would sever them from their Brethren and connect them with aliens?

To the efficacy and permanency of your Union, a Government for the whole is indispensable—No alliances, however strict, between the parts can be an adequate substitute; they must inevitably experience the infractions and interruptions which all alliances in all times have experienced. Sensible of this momentous truth, you have improved upon your first essay, by the adoption of a Constitution of Government better calculated than your former for an intimate Union, and for the efficacious management of your common concerns. This Government, the offspring of our own choice, uninfluenced and unawed, adopted upon full investigation and mature deliberation, completely free in its principles, in the distribution of its powers, uniting security with energy, and containing within itself a provision for its own amendment, has a just claim to your confidence and your support. Respect for its authority, compliance with its laws, acquiescence in its measures, are duties enjoined by the fundamental maxims of true Liberty. The basis of our political systems is the right of the people to make and to alter their Constitutions of Goverment—But, the Constitution which at any time exists, 'till changed by an explicit and authentic act of the whole people, is sacredly obligatory upon all. The very idea of the power and the right of the people to establish Government, presupposes the duty of every individual to obey the established Government.

All obstructions to the execution of the Laws, all combinations and associations, under whatever plausible character, with real design to direct, controul, counteract, or awe the regular deliberation and action of the constituted authorities, are destructive of this fundamental principle, and of fatal tendency. They serve to organize faction, to give it an artificial and extraordinary force—to put in the place of the delegated will of the nation, the will of a party, often a small but artful and enterprizing minority of the community; and, according to the alternate triumphs of different parties, to make the public administration the mirror of the ill-concerted and incongruous projects of faction, rather than the organ of consistent and wholesome plans digested by common councils, and modified by mutual interests.

However combinations or associations of the above description may now and then answer popular ends, they are likely in the course of time and things, to become potent engines, by which cunning, ambitious and unprincipled men will be enabled to subvert the power of the people, and to usurp for themselves the reins of Government; destroying afterwards the very engines which have lifted them to unjust dominion.

Towards the preservation of your Government, and the permanency of your present happy state, it is requisite, not only that you steadily discountenance irregular oppositions to its acknowledged authority, but also that you resist with care the spirit of innovation upon its principles however specious the pretexts.—One method

190

of assault may be to effect in the forms of the constitution alterations which will impair the energy of the system, and thus to undermine what cannot be directly overthrown. In all the changes to which you may be invited, remember that time and habit are at least as necessary to fix the true character of governments, as of other human institutions—that experience is the surest standard, by which to test the real tendency of the existing constitution of a country—that facility in changes upon the credit of mere hypothesis and opinion, exposes to perpetual change, from the endless variety of hypothesis and opinion; and remember, especially, that for the efficient management of your common interest, in a country so extensive as ours, a government of as much vigour as is consistent with the perfect security of liberty, is indispensable. Liberty itself will find in such a government, with powers properly distributed and adjusted, its surest guardian. It is indeed little else than a name, where the government is too feeble to withstand the enterprizes of faction, to confine each member of the society within the limits prescribed by the laws, and so maintain all in the secure and tranquil enjoyment of the rights of person and property.

I have already intimated to you, the danger of parties in the state, with particular reference to the founding of them on geographical discriminations. Let me now take a more comprehensive view, and warn you in the most solemn manner against the baneful effects of the spirit of party, generally.

This spirit, unfortunately, is inseparable from our nature, having its root in the strongest passions of the human mind. It exists under different shapes in all governments more or less stifled, controuled, or repressed; but in those of the popular form, it is seen in its greatest rankness, and is truly their worst enemy.

The alternate domination of one faction over another, sharpened by the spirit of revenge, natural to party dissention, which in different ages and countries has perpetrated the most horrid enormities, is itself a frightful despotism.—But this leads at length to a more formal and permanent despotism.—The disorders and miseries, which result, gradually incline the minds of men to seek security and repose in the absolute power of an individual: and sooner or later the chief of some prevailing faction more able or more fortunate than his competitors, turns this disposition to the purposes of his own elevation, on the ruins of Public Liberty.

Without looking forward to an extremity of this kind (which nevertheless ought not to be entirely out of sight) the common and continual mischiefs of the spirit of party are sufficient to make it the interest and duty of a wise People to discourage and restrain it.

It serves always to distract the Public Councils and enfeeble the Public Administration. It agitates the community with ill-founded jealousies and false alarms; kindles the animosity of one part against another, foments occasionally riot and insurrection. It opens the door to foreign influence and corruption, which find a facilitated access to the government itself through the channels of party passions. Thus the policy and the will of one country are subjected to the policy and will of another.

There is an opinion that parties in free countries are useful checks upon the administration of the Government, and serve to keep alive the spirit of Liberty. This within certain limits is probably true; and in Governments of a Monarchical cast, Patriotism may look with indulgence, if not with favour upon the spirit of party. But in those of the popular character, in Governments purely elective, it is a spirit not to be encouraged. From their natural tendency, it is certain there will always be enough of that spirit for every salutary purpose. And there being constant danger of excess, the effort ought to be, by force of public opinion, to mitigate and assuage it. A fire not to be quenched; it demands a uniform vigilance to prevent its bursting into a flame, lest, instead of warming it should consume.

It is important likewise, that the habits of thinking in a free country, should inspire caution, in those entrusted with its administration, to confine themselves within their respective constitutional spheres, avoiding in the exercise of the powers of one department to encroach upon another. The spirit of encroachment tends to consolidate the powers of all the departments in one, and thus to create, whatever the form of government, a real despotism. A just estimate of that love of power, and proneness to abuse it, which predominates in the human heart, is sufficient to satisfy us of the truth of this position. The necessity of reciprocal checks in the exercise of political power; by dividing and distributing it into different depositories, and constituting each the Guardian of the Public Weal against invasions by the others, has been evinced by experiments ancient and modern: some of them in our country and under our own eyes. To preserve them must be as necessary as to institute them. If, in the opinion of the People, the distribution or modification of the constitutional powers be in any particular wrong, let it be corrected by an amendment in a way which the constitution designates.—But let there be no change by usurpation; for though this, in one instance, may be the instrument of good, it is the customary weapon by which free governments are destroyed.—The precedent must always greatly overbalance in permanent evil any partial or transient benefit which the use can at any time yield.

Of all the dispositions and habits which lead to political prosperity, Religion and Morality are indispensable supports.—In vain would that man claim the tribute of Patriotism, who should labour to subvert these great pillars of human happiness, these firmest props of the duties of Men and Citizens.—The mere Politician, equally with the pious man, ought to respect and to cherish them.— A volume could not trace all their connections with private and publick felicity. Let it simply be asked where is the security for property, for reputation, for life, if the sense of religious obligation *desert* the oaths, which are

194

the instruments of investigation in Courts of Justice? And let us with caution indulge the supposition, that morality can be maintained without religion. Whatever may be conceded to the influence of refined education on minds of peculiar structure; reason and experience both forbid us to expect that national morality can prevail in exclusion of religious principle.

'Tis substantially true, that virtue or morality is a necessary spring of popular government. The rule indeed extends with more or less force to every species of free government. Who that is a sincere friend to it can look with indifference upon attempts to shake the foundation of the fabric?

Promote, then, as an object of primary importance, institutions for the general diffusion of knowledge.—In proportion as the structure of a government gives force to public opinion, it is essential that public opinion should be enlightened.

As a very important source of strength and security, cherish public credit. One method of preserving it is to use it as sparingly as possible; avoiding occasions of expence by cultivating peace, but remembering also that timely disbursements to prepare for danger frequently prevent much greater disbursements to repel it; avoiding likewise the accumulation of debt, not only by shuning occasions of expence, but by vigorous exertions in time of peace to discharge the debts which unavoidable wars may have occasioned, not ungenerously throwing upon posterity the burthen which we ourselves ought to

195

bear.—The execution of these maxims belongs to your representatives, but it is necessary that public opinion should co operate.—To facilitate to them the performance of their duty, it is essential that you should practically bear in mind, that towards the payment of debts there must be revenue: that to have revenue there must be taxes; that no taxes can be devised which are not more or less inconvenient and unpleasant; that the intrinsic embarrassment inseparable from the selection of the proper objects (which is always a choice of difficulties) ought to be a decisive motive for a candid construction of the conduct of the government in making it, and for a spirit of acquiescence in the measures for obtaining revenue which the public exigencies may at any time dictate.

Observe good faith and justice towards all nations, cultivate peace and harmony with all; religion and morality enjoin this conduct; and can it be that good policy does not equally enjoin it? It will be worthy of a free, enlightened, and, at no distant period, a great nation, to give to mankind the magnanimous and too novel example of a people always guided by an exalted justice and benevolence. Who can doubt that in the course of time and things, the fruits of such a plan would richly repay any temporary advantages which might be lost by a steady adherence to it? Can it be, that Providence has not connected the permanent felicity of a nation with its virtue? The experiment, at least, is recommended by every sentiment which ennobles human nature. Alas! is it rendered impossible by its vices!

In the execution of such a plan, nothing is more essential than that permanent, inveterate antipathies against particular nations, and passionate attachments for others, should be excluded; and that in place of them just and amicable feelings towards all should be cultivated. The nation, which indulges towards another an habitual hatred, or an habitual fondness, is in some degree a slave. It is a slave to its animosity or to its affection, either of which is sufficient to lead it astray from its duty and its interest. Antipathy in one nation against another disposes each more readily to offer insult and injury, to lay hold of slight causes of umbrage, and to be haughty and intractable, when accidental or trifling occasions of dispute occur. Hence frequent collisions, obstinate, envenomed and bloody contests. The nation, prompted by ill will and resentment, sometimes impels to war the government, contrary to the best calculations of policy. The government sometimes participates in the national propensity, and adopts through passion what reason would reject; at other times, it makes the animosity of the nation subservient to projects of hostility instigated by pride, ambition, and other sinister and pernicious motives. The peace often, sometimes perhaps the liberty, of nations has been the victim.

So likewise, a passionate attachment of one nation for another produces a variety of evils. Sympathy for the favourite nation, facilitating the illusion of an imaginary common interest, in cases where no real common interest exists, and infusing into one the enmities of the other, betrays the former into a participation in the quarrels and wars of the latter, without adequate inducement or justification. It leads also to concessions to the favourite nations of privileges denied to others, which is apt doubly to injure the nation making the concessions; by unnecessarily parting with what ought to have been retained; and by exciting jealousy, ill will, and a disposition to retaliate, in the parties from whom equal privileges are withheld: And it gives to ambitious, corrupted or deluded citizens (who devote themselves to the favorite nation) facility to betray or sacrifice the interest of their own country, without odium, sometimes even with popularity; gilding with the appearances of a virtuous sense of obligation, a commendable deference for public opinion, or a laudable zeal for public good, the base or foolish compliances of ambition, corruption or infatuation.

As avenues to foreign influence in innumerable ways, such attachments are particularly alarming to the truly enlightened and independent patriot. How many opportunities do they afford to tamper with domestic factions, to practice the arts of seduction, to mislead public opinion, to influence or awe the Public Councils! Such an attachment of a small or weak, towards a great and powerful nation, dooms the former to be the satellite of the latter.

Against the insidious wiles of foreign influence (I conjure you to believe me, fellow-citizens) the jealousy of a free people ought to be *constantly* awake; since history and experience prove that foreign influence is one of the most baneful foes of Republican Government. But that jealousy to be useful must be impartial; else it becomes the instrument of the very influence to be avoided, instead of a defence against it.—Excessive partiality for one foreign nation, and excessive dislike of another, cause those whom they actuate to see danger only on one side, and serve to veil and even to second the arts of influence on the other.—Real patriots, who may resist the intrigues of the favourite, are liable to become suspected and odious; while its tools and dupes usurp the applause and confidence of the people, to surrender their interests.

The great rule of conduct for us, in regard to foreign nations, is in extending our commercial relations, to have with them as little *political* connection as possible. So far as we have already formed engagements, let them be fulfilled with perfect good faith.—Here let us stop.

Europe has a set of primary interests, which to us have none, or a very remote relation. Hence she must be engaged in frequent controversies, the causes of which are essentially foreign to our concerns. Hence, therefore, it must be unwise in us to implicate ourselves, by artificial ties, in the ordinary vicissitudes of her politics, or the ordinary combinations and collisions of her friendships, or enmities.

Our detached and distant situation invites and enables us to pursue a different course. If we remain one people, under an efficient government, the period is not far off, when we may defy material injury from external annoyance: when we may take such an attitude as will cause the neutrality, we may at any time resolve upon, to be scrupulously respected; when belligerent nations, under the impossibility of making acquisitions upon us, will not lightly hazard the giving us provocation; when we may choose peace or war, as our interest, guided by justice, shall counsel.

Why forego the advantages of so peculiar a situation? Why quit our own to stand upon foreign ground? Why, by interweaving our destiny with that of any part of Europe, entangle our peace and prosperity in the toils of European ambition, rivalship, interest, humour or caprice?

'Tis our true policy to steer clear of permanent alliances, with any portion of the foreign world; so far, I mean, as we are now at liberty to do it; for let me not be understood as capable of patronising infidelity to existing engagements. I hold the maxim no less applicable to public than to private affairs, that honesty is always the best policy. I repeat it, therefore, let those engagements be observed in their genuine sense. But in my opinion, it is unnecessary and would be unwise to extend them.

Taking care always to keep ourselves, by suitable establishments, on a respectable defensive posture, we may safely trust to temporary alliances for extraordinary emergencies.

Harmony, liberal intercourse with all nations, are recommended by policy, humanity, and interest. But even our commercial policy should hold an equal and impartial hand; neither seeking nor granting exclusive favours or preferences; consulting the natural course of things; diffusing and diversifying by gentle means the streams of commerce, but forcing nothing; establishing, with powers so disposed, in order to give trade a stable course, to define the rights of our merchants, and to enable the government to support them; conventional rules of intercourse, the best that present circumstances and mutual opinion will permit, but temporary, and liable to be from time to time abandoned or varied, as experience and circumstances, shall dictate; constantly keeping in view, that 'tis folly in one nation to look for disinterested favours from another; that it must pay with a portion of its independence for whatever it may accept under that character; that by such acceptance, it may place itself in the condition of having given equivalents for nominal favours, and yet of being reproached with ingratitude for not giving more. There can be no greater error than to expect, or calculate upon real favours from nation to nation. 'Tis an illusion which experience must cure, which a just pride ought to discard.

In offering to you my countrymen, these counsels of an old and affectionate friend, I dare not hope they will make the strong and lasting impression I could wish; that they will controul the usual current of the passions, or prevent our nation from running the course which has hitherto marked the destiny of nations: But if I may even flatter myself, that they may be productive of some partial benefit, some occasional good; that they may now and then recur to moderate the fury of party spirit, to warn against the mischiefs of foreign intrigue, to guard against the impostures of pretended patriotism; this hope will be a full recompence for the solicitude of your welfare, by which they have been dictated.

How far in the discharge of my official duties, I have been guided by the principles that have been delineated, the public records and other evidences of my conduct must witness to you and to the world. To myself, the assurance of my own conscience is, that I have at least believed myself to be guided by them.

In relation to the still subsisting war in Europe, my proclamation of the 22d of April, 1793, is the index to my Plan. Sanctioned by your approving voice and by that of your Representatives in both Houses of Congress, the spirit of that measure has continually governed me; uninfluenced by any attempts to deter or divert me from it.

After deliberate examination with the aid of the best lights I could obtain, I was well satisfied that our country, under all the circumstances of the case, had a right to take, and was bound in duty and interest, to take a neutral position. Having taken it, I determined, as far as should depend upon me, to maintain it, with moderation, perseverance and firmness.

The considerations which respect the right to hold this conduct, it is not necessary on this occasion to detail. I will only observe, that according to my understanding of the matter, that right, so far from being denied by any of the Belligerent Powers, has been virtually admitted by all.

The duty of holding a neutral conduct may be inferred, without any thing more, from the obligations which justice and humanity impose on every nation, in cases in which it is free to act, to maintain inviolate the relations of peace and amity towards other nations.

The inducements of interest for observing that conduct will best be referred to your own reflections and experience. With me, a predominant motive has been to endeavour to gain time to our country to settle and mature its yet recent institutions, and to progress without interruption, to that degree of strength and consistency, which is necessary to give it, humanly speaking, the command of its own fortunes.

Though in reviewing the incidents of my administration, I am unconscious of intentional error: I am nevertheless too sensible of my defects not to think it probable that I may have committed many errors. Whatever they may be, I fervently beseech the Almighty to avert or mitigate the evils to which they may tend. I shall also carry with me the hope that my Country will never cease to view them with indulgence; and that after forty-five years of my life dedicated to its service, with an upright zeal, the faults of incompetent abilities will be consigned to oblivion, as myself must soon be to the mansions of rest.

Relying on its kindness in this as in other things, and actuated by that fervent love towards it, which is so natural to a man, who views in it the native soil of himself and his progenitors for several generations; I anticipate with pleasing expectation that retreat, in which I promise myself to realize, without alloy, the sweet enjoyment of partaking, in the midst of my fellow Citizens, the benign influence of good laws under a free government—the ever favourite object of my heart, and the happy reward, as I trust, of our mutual cares, labours and dangers.

GEORGE WASHINGTON

APPENDIX B

Speech of Patrick Henry before the House of Burgesses
1775

Mr. President, No man thinks more highly than I do of the patriotism, as well as abilities, of the very worthy gentlemen who have just addressed the house. But different men often see the same subject in different lights; and, therefore, I hope it will not be thought disrespectful to those gentlemen if, entertaining, as I do, opinions of a character very opposite to theirs, I shall speak forth my sentiments freely and without reserve. This is no time for ceremony. The question before the house is one of awful moment to this country. For my own part, I consider it as nothing less than a question of freedom or slavery; and in proportion to the magnitude of the subject ought to be the freedom of the debate. It is only in this way that we can hope to arrive at truth, and fulfill the great responsibility which we hold to God and our country. Should I keep back my opinions at such a time, through fear of giving offence, I should consider myself as guilty of treason towards my country, and of an act of disloyalty towards the majesty of Heaven, which I revere above all earthly kings.

Mr. President, it is natural to man to indulge in the illusions of hope. We are apt to shut our eyes against a painful truth, and listen to the song of that siren, till she transforms us into beasts. Is this the part of wise men, engaged in a great and arduous struggle for liberty? Are we disposed to be of the number of those who, having eyes, see not, and having ears, hear not, the things which so nearly concern their temporal salvation? For my part, whatever anguish of spirit it may cost, I am willing to know the whole truth; to know the worst and to provide for it.

I have but one lamp by which my feet are guided, and that is the lamp of experience. I know of no way of judging of the future but by the past. And judging by the past, I wish to know what there has been in the conduct of the British ministry for the last ten years to justify those hopes with which gentlemen have been pleased to solace themselves and the house? Is it that insidious smile with which our petition has been lately received? Trust it not, sir. It will prove a snare to your feet. Suffer not yourselves to be betrayed with a kiss. Ask yourselves how this gracious reception of our petition comports with those warlike preparations which cover our waters and darken our land. Are fleets and armies necessary to a work of love and reconciliation? Have we shown ourselves so unwilling to be reconciled that force must be called in to win back our love? Let us not deceive ourselves, sir. These are the implements of war and subjugation; the last arguments to which kings resort. I ask gentlemen, sir, what means this martial array, if its purpose be not to force us to submission? Can gentlemen assign any other possible motive for it? Has Great Britain any enemy, in this quarter of the world, to call for all this accumulation of navies and armies? No, sir, she has none. They are meant for us; they can be meant for no other. They are sent over to bind and rivet upon us those chains which the British ministry have been so long forging. And what have we to oppose to them? Shall we try argument? Sir, we have been trying that for the last ten years. Have we anything new to offer upon the subject? Nothing. We have held the subject up in every light of which it is capable; but it has all been in vain. Shall we resort to entreaty and humble supplication? What terms shall we find which have not been already exhausted? Let us not, I beseech you, sir, deceive ourselves longer. Sir, we have done everything that could be done to avert the storm which is now coming on. We have petitioned; we have remonstrated; we have supplicated; we have prostrated ourselves before the throne, and have implored its interposition to arrest the tyrannical hands of the ministry and Parliament. Our petitions have been slighted; our remonstrances have produced additional violence and insult; our supplications have been disregarded, and we have been spurned with contempt, from the foot of the throne! In vain, after these things, may we indulge the fond hope of peace and reconciliation. There is no longer any room for hope. If we wish to be free; if we mean to preserve inviolate those inestimable privileges for which we have been so long contending; if we mean not basely to abandon the noble struggle in which we have been so long engaged, and which we have pledged ourselves never to abandon, until the glorious object of our contest shall be obtained, we must fight! I repeat it, sir, we must fight! An appeal to arms and to the God of Hosts is all that is left us!

They tell us, sir, that we are weak; unable to cope with so formidable an adversary. But when shall we be stronger? Will it be the next week or the next year? Will it be when we are totally disarmed, and when a British guard shall be stationed in every house? Shall we gather strength by irresolution and inaction? Shall we acquire the means of effectual resistance by lying supinely on our backs and hugging the delusive phantom of hope, until our enemies shall have bound us hand and foot? Sir, we are not weak, if we make a proper use of those means which the God of nature hath placed in our power. Three millions of people, armed in the holy cause of liberty, and in such a country as that which we possess, are invincible by any force which our enemy can send against us. Besides, sir, we shall not fight our battles alone. There is a just God who presides over the destinies of nations, and who will raise up friends to fight our battles for us. The battle, sir, is not to the strong alone; it is to the vigilant, the active, the brave. Besides, sir, we have no election. If we were base enough to desire it, it is now too late to retire from the contest. There is no retreat, but in submission and slavery! Our chains are forged! Their clanking may be heard on the plains of Boston! The war is inevitable—and let it come. I repeat it, sir, let it come.

It is vain, sir, to extenuate the matter. Gentlemen may cry, Peace, peace—but there is no peace. The war is actually begun! The next gale that sweeps from the north will bring to our ears the clash of resounding arms! Our brethren are already in the field! Why stand we here idle? What is it that gentlemen wish? What would they have? Is life so dear, or peace so sweet, as to be purchased at the price of chains and slavery? Forbid it, Almighty God! I know not what course others may take; but as for me, give me liberty or give me death!

PATRICK HENRY

The Liberty or Death Speech. On March 23, 1775, he offered resolutions in the Richmond convention to organize the militia and put the colony in a state of defence. The resolutions met with great opposition, and in supporting them he made the above address.

NOTES

CHAPTER I

1. Abraham Lincoln, speaking in Springfield, Illinois, on January 27, 1837. The full text of this speech can be found in the Gettysburg Edition of *Lincoln's Complete Works* (New York, Francis D. Tandy & Company, 1905), Vol. I, p. 37.

CHAPTER II

1. For an illuminating account of recent conditions of United States gold reserves, see *U.S. News & World Report* (December 28, 1959). See also an article by Michael Stephan, "Is The Gold Crisis For The United States Now Inevitable?" in *The Magazine of Wall Street* (May 23, 1959).

2. Mr. Dulles is quoted to this effect in a speech by the Honorable John G. Diefenbaker, Prime Minister of Canada, to the Pilgrim Society, October 28, 1958.

3. The full text of President Washington's Farewell Address is in Appendix A.

4. Charles Callan Tansill, author of *Back Door to War: Roosevelt Foreign Policy, 1933-1941,* is a professor of American diplomatic history at Georgetown University in Washington, D.C. He is a brilliant and respected historian who has written eleven

books on American diplomatic history from 1921 until 1946. They include *America Goes to War* (1938) and *The Foreign Policy of Thomas F. Bayard* (1940).

5. General Albert C. Wedemeyer, author of *Wedemeyer Reports!*, is a West Point graduate. He has had experience in both military and political affairs. In 1936, he was assigned to the German War College in Berlin for two years. On his return, he joined the War Plans Division of the U.S. General Staff. He attended world conferences in London, Washington, Casablanca, Cairo, and Quebec with General George C. Marshall. In 1943, he was assigned to the Southeast Asia Command with Admiral Mountbatten. In 1944, he relieved General Stillwell as theater commander in China.

6. Holmes Alexander is the Washington commentator, and the quotation used here is from his column for November 6, 1958.

7. *Wall Street Journal*, July 21, 1958.

CHAPTER III

1. Verse by Richard Armour quoted in the *American Economic Review*.

2. During the months of September and October, 1958, Nina and Gene Pulliam toured the Middle East. The Pulliams are one of the most widely read reporting teams in the United States. They have reported jointly from eighty-four countries in which they interviewed a wide variety of native and American experts. Copies of their series of articles entitled "Are We Too Late in the Middle East?" can be obtained in booklet form from the Public Relations departments of the *Arizona Republic* and the *Indianapolis Star*. As a result of the republication of the Pulliams' articles on Turkey by Turkish editor Ahmet Emin Yalman in his Istanbul newspaper *Vatan*, seventy-two year old Yalman was imprisoned under Turkish laws which forbid a newspaper to "insult" the government. His release in April, 1960, resulted from a doctor's warning that he had heart trouble.

3. Vermont Royster, Pulitzer Prize-winning editor of the *Wall Street Journal*, spent several months traveling and reporting in Southeast Asia. This quote, from one of a series of articles which appeared in the *Wall Street Journal* under the title "Anatomy of an Aid Program," appeared on the editorial page of the *Wall Street Journal* on April 9, 1959.

4. For a more complete account of the situation in the nationalized tin mines of Bolivia, see *Latin American Report* (December, 1958).

5. From *Foreign Aid Construction Projects,* the twenty-ninth report by the House Committee on Government Operations (*House Report No. 2012*).

6. Malcolm Muggeridge, quoted in a column by Michael Padev, foreign editor of the *Indianapolis Star,* April 30, 1959.

7. From General George C. Marshall's speech at Harvard, June 6, 1947, when he announced the Marshall Plan.

8. Speech by Senator Harry F. Byrd of Virginia on the floor of the United States Senate. See the *Congressional Record* of May 14, 1958, p. 7836.

CHAPTER IV

1. For a more complete account of men like Paul Rusch, see *Life* (December 7, 1959).

2. Thomas A. Dooley, *The Edge of Tomorrow,* (New York, Berkley Publishing Corp., 1958), p. 142.

3. See *Time* (November 30, 1959) for an interesting account of India's food problem. See also P. T. Bauer, *United States Aid and Indian Economic Development* (Washington, American Enterprise Association, 1959).

CHAPTER V

1. See "Exaggerated Rubles Mask Soviet Failures," by Alice Widener, *Indianapolis Star,* February 1, 1959.

2. For additional material on Soviet foreign trade, see "Foreign Trade as an Instrument of Soviet Policy," prepared by the Soviet Affairs Analysis Service, Institute for the Study of the USSR, Munich, Germany.

CHAPTER VI

1. This quotation from Churchill appears in Vice-President Nixon's article on the late John Foster Dulles in the June 2, 1959, issue of *Life.*

2. Edgar Ansel Mowrer, in a column reprinted in *ACEN News* (April, 1959), published by the Assembly of Captive European Nations.

3. The original text of Patrick Henry's speech is in Appendix B.

CHAPTER VII

1. One day, Charlie Blum, a stereotyper who works for the *Star,* came into my office, as he often does, to discuss current events and the state of the world. During the course of our conversation, he mentioned Martin Koszta and the Hulseman Letter. I had not heard of this incident before, so I decided to look it up. The *Encyclopaedia Britannica* did not list it, and the *Encyclopedia Americana* had only a short account. So I got out the 1909 edition of *Nelson's Encyclopaedia* to find the details on which the story is based. The incident deserves wider attention than it has received.

2. John Noble was in Germany at the outbreak of World War II and was interned by the Nazis. In 1945, he was seized by the invading Russians and sent to a Soviet slave-labor camp north of Moscow, in Arctic Russia. He saw a revolt of Soviet prisoners break out at Vorkuta, where he was held captive. No charges were ever placed against him by the Soviets, and he was not told why he was released, after more than nine years of imprisonment, in December, 1954. Associated Press wire stories in December, 1954, and January, 1955, describe his experiences.

3. On April 26, 1951, William Oatis, Bureau Chief of the Associated Press in Prague, disappeared. On June 14, 1951, he was charged with writing dispatches "hostile to the state" by the Communist Czech government. On July 5, he was sentenced to ten years in prison. This was two days after two American jet pilots landed, by error, in Czechoslovakia, where they were seized but later ransomed by the United States. Congressman John Beamer of Indiana, Oatis' native state, repeatedly charged that the State Department's lack of protest and "apparent indifference" were responsible for Oatis' continued imprisonment. For a time the Czech government tried to extract ransom from the United States government in the form of acknowledgment of title to an American-owned steel mill that had been taken over by the Communists. No reprisals of any kind were undertaken against the Czech government by the United States, although a substantial body of public opinion and a considerable number of legislators demanded such action. Oatis was finally released May 15, 1953, and is now working with the AP Bureau in the United Nations.

4. Robert A. Vogeler, former executive of the International

Telephone & Telegraph Corporation, was assigned in 1948 to negotiate with the Communist government of Hungary about the status of property owned by I.T.&T. He was arrested in Budapest on November 29, 1949, and charged with espionage for the United States. After undergoing repeated brainwashings at the hands of Communist officials, he signed a "confession." During his imprisonment, the State Department made several protests and publicly decried the actions of the Hungarian government, but no retaliatory action was taken. Vogeler was released, after his "confession," on April 17, 1951, and at once repudiated all statements made by him or reported to have been made by him while he was in Communist hands. It seems probable that he was imprisoned chiefly to extract the "confession" and "prove" for public consumption the Communist charges of American espionage in Communist nations.

5. Four American noncommissioned officers—Army Sgt. Dale M. McCuistion, Air Force T/Sgt. James D. King, Air Force S/Sgt. Giacomo Recevuto, and Air Force Sgt. Joseph Proietti—were tried in Turkish courts for alleged black-market operations. These men, regardless of their guilt or innocence, were under American military authority when seized and were subject to American military discipline. They had been sent to Turkey by the United States government; they were not there of their own free will. Yet under the Status of Forces Treaty with Turkey, they were turned over to Turkish authorities and tried under Turkish laws. Many other cases of this kind have occurred, in Japan and elsewhere, where similar treaties are in force.

6. *Newsweek* (December 7, 1959), p. 30.

7. Arizona Senator Barry Goldwater wrote to Bunche protesting the treatment of Bang-Jensen. He received a letter from Bunche dated June 25, 1958, in which Bunche said: "I may inform you that Mr. Bang-Jensen is under suspension and the Secretary General has under consideration a recommendation of the United Nations Joint Disciplinary Committee for his termination on the basis of a number of charges. You will appreciate that for the good of the individual involved we do not make public the nature of such charges and of personnel actions, which are purely internal matters. I may again assure you, however, that there is no foundation for the reports you have cited.

Ralph J. Bunche
Under Secretary"

Chapter VIII

1. See the *Congressional Record* of August 22, 1958, for the report of the American Bar Association's Special Committee To Study Communist Tactics, Strategy and Objectives. The Committee, under Chairman Herbert R. O'Conor, submitted its report at the annual meeting of the American Bar Association held at London in July, 1957.

2. G. Warren Nutter, "The True Story of Russia's Weakness," *U.S. News & World Report* (March 1, 1957). Professor Nutter was the director of a study of Soviet economic growth made by the National Bureau of Economic Research under the sponsorship of the Rockefeller Foundation. Additional material is from his paper, "Soviet Industrial Achievements: A Summary," which was read to the Mont Pelerin Society at Oxford, England, in September, 1959. There is additional material on this subject in "The Crisis of Soviet Capitalism," *Fortune* (February, 1959).

3. Edward R. Murrow warned the American public about the dangers of the Seven Year Plan in a radio broadcast the week of November 17, 1958.

A brief study of the reasons for the abandonment of the Sixth Five Year Plan was made by the Soviet Affairs Analysis Service (see Note 2, Chapter V), and its findings were released on January 27, 1959. The study reveals, among other things, Soviet failures to achieve increased production in five basic industries:

	Planned	*Actual '56*	*Actual '57*	*Estimated '58*
Steel	4.6 million tons	3.3	2.4	2.6
Pig Iron	3.9 "	2.5	1.2	2.1
Rolled Iron	3.6 "	2.5	2.4	2.5
Coal	40.6 "	28.0	16.8	26.0
Electricity	30.6 " kwh	21.9	17.5	21.0

Says the study: "This record of those branches of industry on which all expansion depends has been, in the first three years of the Sixth Five Year Plan, one of failure. This failure is one which can bring with it failure of the entire plan, which, like all current Soviet planning, is predicated on the primacy of heavy industry over consumer goods. To avoid such a failure, which might well prove catastrophic to the Soviet regime as constituted at present, the Sixth Five Year Plan was scrapped and a new and more grandiose plan (and, it should be noted, one whose results will not be evident for another four or five years) introduced."

4. Mr. Padev wrote a brilliant series of articles examining the economic, political, military, and diplomatic facts about the Soviet Union. These articles have been incorporated into a booklet entitled "The Three Faces of Russia" and can be obtained from the Public Relations Department of the *Indianapolis Star*.

5. Wing Commander Asher Lee of the British Royal Air Force is a British intelligence officer with a world-wide reputation in top military circles for his books on air power. His latest work is *The Soviet Air and Rocket Forces*. He has served on special military missions to the United States and has represented Great Britain at military conferences with the Russians.

A more recent estimate of the comparative power in military strength of the Soviet Union and the United States is in the February 15, 1960, issue of *U.S. News & World Report*: "Is U.S. or Russia Stronger—Answer from a British Expert," by J. M. Mackintosh, advisor to the Institute of Strategic Studies in London. Mackintosh was a British liaison officer attached to the Soviet military command in the Balkans during World War II. He speaks fluent Russian and served as interpreter when Khrushchev and Bulganin visited Great Britain in 1956. His conclusion is that "the deterrent of U.S. long-range nuclear power has never been more effective toward Russia than at this moment."

6. For further information on this document, privately drafted and circulated by top military officials, see *Newsweek* (July 20, 1959).

7. This information about the Jupiter and Redstone missiles in operation in Europe was given by von Braun to the Cleveland post of the American Ordnance Association in an address on January 25, 1960. The address has been reprinted by the Association in booklet form.

8. For a complete rundown on the numbers and stations of American missile systems, see *U.S. News & World Report* (February 22 and February 29, 1960). These articles are based on testimony before Congress by top American military leaders.

9. For fuller treatment of China today than is possible in this book, see Wiznitzer's copyrighted article, "I Saw Red China from the Inside," in the June 15, 1959, issue of *U.S. News & World Report*.

10. Robert Strausz-Hupé, director of the Foreign Policy Research Institute, is one of four authors of a book, *Protracted Con-*

flict, on the strategy and tactics of the Communist cold war against the West. The other authors are William R. Kintner, James E. Dougherty, and Alvin J. Cottrell. This short but very perceptive book will be worth your reading if you want to know why the Communists keep winning the cold war while we have all the military and economic advantages.

CHAPTER IX

1. All of this testimony is contained in a series of reports by the House Un-American Activities Committee entitled *The Crimes of Khrushchev*. The Lebed and Dobriansky testimony was in Part 1, the testimony of Kiraly and Koevago in Part 2. The entire series of reports on Khrushchev's crimes can be obtained from the Committee on Un-American Activities of the House of Representatives, Washington, D.C.

2. I obtained a complete copy of this speech by Khrushchev from an official of the German government in Bonn, Germany, in September, 1959. The complete speech was reported on March 27 of that year by Tass, the Soviet news service.

3. Robert Morris was quoted by the Associated Press, April 1, 1959. The editorial was in the *Indianapolis Star*, April 2, 1959.

4. R. E. Troper, *American Mercury* (November, 1959).

5. *Ibid.*

6 Ambassador Lodge was quoted at the final session of the United Nations by the Associated Press, December 15, 1958.

7. Sir Leslie Munroe, "Can the United Nations Enforce Peace?" *Foreign Affairs* (January, 1960).

8. Frank Crane, editorial writer for the *Indianapolis Star*.

CHAPTER X

1. This is a quotation from Edith Hamilton, one of the world's leading authorities on Greco-Roman civilization. At the age of ninety, she was made an honorary citizen of Athens, Greece, in recognition of her devotion and scholarship in this field. The source of the quote is an article, "The Lessons of the Past," in the *Saturday Evening Post* (September 27, 1958). For an illuminating excursion into these two great past civilizations read her three beautifully written books, *The Echo of Greece, The Greek Way*, and *The Roman Way*. How well the words and deeds of the ancient Greeks apply today is seen in this quotation

from Pericles quoted by Thucydides in his story of the Peloponnesian War. Said Pericles: "Happiness lies in freedom; freedom, however, lies in courage."

2. Part of a letter from Lincoln to Horace Greeley, editor of the *New York Tribune,* dated August 22, 1862. The entire letter can be found in the Gettysburg Edition of *Lincoln's Complete Works.*

3. Quoted by Carlos P. Romulo, *Friend to Friend* (New York, John Day, 1958).

4. Hutchinson wrote me from Cairo on December 19, 1958. These words seemed very prophetic, and most of what he predicted has already come true.

5. This quotation is from a Bell syndicated column by Dorothy Thompson dated August 11, 1958. During the years just before the outbreak of World War II, Miss Thompson repeatedly warned of the dangers inherent in Hitler's rise to power. Like Cassandra, she went unheeded. She has proved, however, that her foresight is almost uncanny. She is an extraordinarily perceptive student of international affairs.

In her column, Miss Thompson said: "Throughout the East the Russian-led bloc is succeeding far better than the bloc led by the United States. . . . The cause of Russia's successes lies in her clearer analysis of the social and political forces moving in the former colonial world and applying the analysis. . . . Russian leaders during and after World War II saw that they could not extend power by the promotion of their 'ideology.'

"What they foresaw, however, was the breakdown of colonialism in Asia and Africa, as the certain result of the two great wars, and the rise of nationalisms which, regardless of ideologies, would support each other and gravitate toward whatever great power would protect and support them. Russia, which never had colonies in the area, has chosen, under Khrushchev, to be that power."

Warped as Soviet interpretations of history may be, they are at least based on serious factual study of the history of nations and civilizations. Apparently, American foreign-policy makers do not take the trouble to try to understand historical, cultural, and strategic truths before deciding on how to deal with the East.

Speaking of foreign aid, Miss Thompson also wrote, on July 24, 1957: "Any great nation whose 'security' (whatever that may mean) depends upon dependents has forfeited its freedom of action and therewith its basic security. Great states must depend upon themselves."